The Universal Soul

Chris Thomas

www.capallbann.co.uk

The Universal Soul

©Copyright Chris Thomas 2005

ISBN 186163 273 8

ALL RIGHTS RESERVED

Cover design by Paul Mason

Published by:

Capall Bann Publishing
Auton Farm
Milverton
Somerset
TA4 1NE

Contents

Also by Chris Thomas, published by Capal Bann:

The Fool's First Steps

The Journey Home

Planet Earth

The Healing Book (With Diane Baker)

Everything You Wanted To Know About Your Body, But So Far Nobody's Been Able To Tell You (With Diane Baker)

The Sequel To Everything (With Diane Baker)

Sam: It's like in the great stories, Mr Frodo, the ones that really mattered. Full of darkness and danger, they were and, sometimes, you didn't want to know the end because how can the end be happy? How could the world go back to the way it was when so much bad happened? But in the end, it is only a passing thing, a shadow. Even darkness must pass, a new day will come and, when the sun shines, it will shine out the clearer.

Those were the stories that stayed with you, that meant something, even if you were too young to understand why. But I think, Mr Frodo, I do understand, I know why. I know now folk in those stories had lots of chances of turning back, but they didn't. They kept going because they were holding on to something.

Frodo: What are we holding on to Sam?

Sam: That there is something good in this world, Mr Frodo, and it is worth fighting for.

Conversation between Frodo Baggins and Samwise Gamgee
From the movie version of JRR Tolkien's 'The Two Towers'.
Words spoken by Elijah Woods as Frodo Baggins and
Sean Astin as Sam-wise Gamgie
See author's note.

This book expresses the beliefs of the author and many of the people who will come into contact with it. There are those however, who will disagree with it. This is called, 'freedom of speech' and 'freedom of choice'.

"...If we all embrace our own truths and express those truths honestly, there will be no more conflict and our transition will be smooth and simple."

Introduction

Curiosity, this is how life begins.

A curiosity along the lines of 'what if?' Together with the energy potential to imbue a lifeless void with the souls who are to explore the 'what if' on behalf of the one who asked the question.

With sufficient energy potential, any question can be asked.

The next question is where?

The nearest analogy would be a cartoonist's 'thought bubble', an envelope of energy into which the energy potential can be generated and contained.

As other thoughts occur, other 'what ifs', new envelopes are added until curiosity is satisfied and new thoughts can be given free reign and explored to their conclusions.

So far, a total of eleven 'thoughts' have been brought into active exploration. Eleven Universes each imbued with the energy potential to answer the Creator's questions.

Our Universe explores the 'what if' of freedom of choice. Every soul that exists within this Universe has the right to choose their own actions, their own directions. The only 'law' that applies is that no one can choose to act in such a way as to remove the free choice of another's free choice to act.

All choose freely without limitations. The Creator does not dictate or interfere in the choices each makes. There would be little point in creating a universe where freedom of choice is the 'what if' being explored and then take away freedom of choice by directing the soul's activities.

Part of the 'what if' of this Universe was also to explore the possibility of fully 'physical' beings being created. This exploration of the physical has led to the existence of the Earth and all of the life that our Earth supports – a miracle of creation. Nowhere, throughout the whole of creation, does an abundance and joy for life exist to the extent it does on Earth. There have been many trials and tribulations throughout our Universe and some of these events have brought the whole 'thought' to a point of near destruction. One thing has sustained this Universe above all else: the Earth must be saved at virtually any cost.

With humanity finally finding the answers to a question we asked ourselves twenty thousand years ago, we are beginning to move forwards into a new phase of existence and this process of change is having an effect on the Universal energies that is beyond our full understanding.

As we move into our new state of being, very many questions arise within each individual. This book is a deeper exploration of the Akashic to try and find the answers and brings *The Journey Home, The Fool's First Steps* and *Planet Earth – The Universe's Experiment* fully up to date.

Chapter One

The First Attempt at Humanity

There is a time when all things come to their end. The 'what ifs' arrive at the point where the answer is known.

This is Earth. The question of humanity has arrived at the point where the answer is known and the final act of the Human Plan can be played out.

This is not still a 'what if' but the culmination of twenty thousand years of searching for the answers to the problems that led to the destruction of a continent and the end of human existence with Atlantis. The new start all of those centuries ago has led us to the current point in human affairs and human development.

Karma, the last seven thousand years of knowledge gathering, has come to fruition and the knowledge of how to be human on this amazing Earth has been won.

But, what to do with this knowledge? In what direction do we take ourselves now? Or is understanding the problem sufficient knowledge for the Creator's purpose and we should leave the Earth as the experiment is complete?

These are some of the questions that humanity needs to answer before the time we allotted to our task finally runs out with the ending of 2011.

2005 is bringing with it a huge impetus for change. The energy structures put into place at the start of 2005 brought with them enough power to change everything that we, humans, have known. Our ability to hide behind our false realities has finally been stripped away and we have to face ourselves and our actions in the full light of a new dawn.

Yes, we really have been as bad as our history shows us to be. We have missed so many opportunities to change, so many opportunities to understand, so many opportunities to remember who we are and what our purpose is. So much of what could have been has been irretrievably lost along the way.

But, we are where we are and it is no good regretting past actions, we just need to put our final piece of knowledge gathering into its proper context.

As these new energies began to take form at the end of 2004, new areas of knowledge and information began to be added into the record keeping aspect of the human mass consciousness, the Akashic, that can help to take away the sense of missed opportunities and allow us to review our human past with a slightly different point of view. This new knowledge does not fully exonerate us from our past but it does allow us a fresh perspective so that our final decisions are not based upon unknowing guilt.

Human existence began on Earth eighty five thousand years ago with the genetic acceleration of Cro Magnon man into Homo Sapien Sapien (the name is that given to humans by scientists. It means Homo – man, Sapien – wise. Scientific arrogance at its worst).

On Atlantis, we were so much more than we, today, are used to being. We had the whole of the soul within the physical. There was not the division between the 'physical self' and the 'higher self' that we have become so accustomed to over the past few thousand years. We had complete psychic communication with all living things. We could communicate across the planet to each other or we could communicate, in a two-way conversation, with a blade of grass. The entire planet was open to us and our psychic awareness was at its peak.

It is difficult to describe who and what we were at this time in our history. Our limited five senses cannot even begin to approach full psychic awareness. Our disconnected senses can be likened to single notes within the orchestral symphony that is full awareness. Our vocabulary is based upon knowledge gained from our limited sensory experiences and so words cannot be used to give even a glimpse of what complete psychic awareness means.

If, for example, we take a look at a shark. Any species of shark will do, they share many common attributes. A shark has sensory organs that run along their flanks. These sensory receptors allow a shark to detect movement in water up to one metre away. This means that its prey can be out of sight but can still be detected in the water around the shark. A shark can also detect one drop of blood in seawater up to three kilometres away. Humans do not have these kinds of senses. We cannot detect near movement; neither can we 'smell' up to three kilometres. To the shark, it is all perfectly natural, it is a part of its fundamental make-up, and because it is such a fundamental part of its make-up, it cannot describe what it is like to have these kinds of senses. Humans have become blind, bound and senseless in these kinds of terms and, ultimately, it was our choice to do so.

We have not become this unaware by accident. There are two reasons why our sensory deprivation has arisen.

Firstly, we began to lose who we were, what our origins are and our lack of understanding of the process of being human followed. This was brought about by forces and processes we did not understand. Secondly, once we had begun to understand that problems did exist, we deliberately chose to limit our view and understanding so that we could learn how to climb back to where we once were.

To explain these statements, we have to go back to the time of Atlantis.

The Universe we live within is one that explores the 'what if' of absolute freedom of choice. That means that each individual soul, be that galaxy, planet, individual or even rock, has the available energies to determine its own course of actions and, consequently, experiences. The only limiting factor is that an individual cannot act in such a way as to remove the free choices made by another individual soul. Freedom of choice is absolute.

Within this concept, this 'what if', was one clear question from the Creator – is human life possible?

Throughout the whole of Creation, life exists at either non-physical levels or at semi-physical levels. Non-physical means beings that exist at energy frequencies where they have no 'physical' density; they just exist in a pure energy form. Shape without what we would call density. Pure soul energy in a roughly human form, what most would romantically call 'Angels'.

Semi-physicals are a range of beings that have a 'physical' density but are not 'solid', as we would define the term. To each other, the semi-physical races see themselves as being as 'physical' as one human would see another. We would only 'see' some aspects of these beings as our brains are tuned to frequencies that only exist within the 'physical' spectrum of energies. To us, these semi-physical beings would appear as an outline comprised of transparent energies but without fine details.

The 'request' from the Creator to this Universe was to find out if 'physical' life could exist, bearing in mind freedom of choice. The first time we attempted to fulfil this request, we felt that we had failed and our choice was to begin again. The whole Universe was collapsed and the process was begun again from the beginning.

As soon as the new Universe, our current one, was established and fully functional, we set about forming a region of space where the possibility of 'physical' life could be attempted.

The non-physical races live in any region of space they choose. They do not require any form of 'food' as they take what little nourishment they need directly from the free flowing energy patterns that exist everywhere throughout the Universe.

The semi-physical races are a little different though. To provide their 'physical' forms, they require that space is 'compressed' into a particular collection of energy frequencies. This is achieved by forming an energy 'bubble' like a rugby ball in shape, a miniature Universe in its own right. Each of the seven regions formed in this way contain their own mix of energy frequencies which provide characteristic form and size to the 'bubble's' inhabitants. Size, shape and energy 'signature' are created in this way. Form follows frequency.

The energy 'bubbles' surrounding these regions of space are large enough to contain several galaxies. This gives these races ample opportunity to colonise other worlds in order to experience and learn. As they require food and an atmosphere in much the same way as we do, they needed to develop ships that protected and nurtured them in order for them to explore. Their energy structures were designed to encourage them to adapt and to explore everything around them and several of these races developed an ability to travel between galaxies several million years ago. Six of the seven semi-physical races now have the ability to travel across a number of galaxies.

The seventh race have no need of physical travel as they are crystalline in form and have no need to physically move let alone travel beyond their planet. Their mode of exploration is through their ability to consciously project themselves anywhere they wish within the Universal whole.

These semi-physical races are described in detail in later chapters where their story has interwoven with ours so this is a very brief description for those unfamiliar with these races.

This list is given in no particular order.

The Pleiadeans

These are a race that originate on the star system we call the Pleiades. This name for the star system is the one the Pleiadeans gave to it themselves and we adopted it when we first began to record information of this nature.

In form, the Pleiadeans are closest to the human shape. They tend to be about 2.4m (8ft) tall with features similar to a Nordic race as well as being blond and blue eyed. They tend to become involved in most activities that take place throughout the Universe.

The Sirians

For the same reasons as the Pleiadeans, we call this race Sirians as they originate on the star system Sirius.

The Sirians tend to be 1.7m-1.9m (5ft 8ins to 6ft) tall. They are grey skinned with very slim bodies, arms and legs. Their eyes are very dark and quite large with the other facial features not very well defined. The Sirians have taken on a 'technical' role within the Universe and so become involved with most activities.

The NGC 584

We do not have a name for this race other than an astronomer's catalogue number. This star system is located within the arc of the stars that make up the Pleiadean constellation but is very many galaxies beyond the Pleiades.

They are very similar in form to a two year old human child, about 90cm (2ft 6ins) tall with their heads slightly larger in proportion to their bodies. They have a red/brown skin colour with a leathery texture. They are master geneticists and have been involved with the development of the Earth since the beginning of life.

The Velon

This race calls themselves Velon and originating on a star system they call Velus. This system is situated behind the constellation of Sagittarius and is about thirty five galaxies distant.

They are about 2.4m (8ft) tall with comparatively small heads. They have only recently developed the capability of inter-galactic travel.

The 'Greys'

These are the classic 'aliens', the short grey beings with big black eyes. They originate on a star system that is located behind the constellation of Draco but is seventy galaxies further away.

The are about 1m (3ft) tall with the characteristic grey skin and slender bodies. They do not actually have black eyes but have yellow eyes with vertical irises. The reason for the black appearance of their eyes is given later.

The 'Blues'

Again, their home star system is too distant for us to have named it or even catalogued it. It is located behind the constellation of Capricorn and is forty galaxies distant. They are called the 'Blues', as they are covered in short blue hairs. They are about 1m (3ft) tall with very short legs and round bodies. They frequently travel with the 'Greys'.

The crystalline race makes up the seventh of the semi-physical races.

Three, in particular, of these semi-physical races, (Pleiadeans, NGC 584 and the Sirians) have developed ways of travelling far beyond their original energy 'bubbles' and have developed abilities where they can travel to anywhere within the Universal void regardless of the energy patterns and structures they encounter along the way. These three races have played an immense role in the development of our Earth and the life upon the planet.

One of the functions of this Universe is to explore the possibility of developing life at the kind of physical densities we encounter on Earth. To put this possibility into practical action, a region of space was chosen that was well away from the flows of Universal life.

An energy envelope was constructed which contained the combination of energy frequencies that amount to 'physical densities'. In other words, the energy patterns from which our solar system 'bubble' is constructed contains energy frequencies which condense 'space' down to compaction levels that correspond to 'physical' existence. This bubble of ours contains two hundred and ninety three dimensions of energy. It is this two hundred and ninety three dimensional limit that holds the solar system, and its inhabitants, within the physical realms. Outside of our solar system, other energy frequency collections exist which create other bubbles of possibility.

Between these bubbles, energy potential is infinite. Or at least, as infinite as the energy potential of this Universe. In numerical terms, this Universal infinity extends to 38 x 10 to the power of 32,000 dimensions. That is, thirty eight with thirty two thousand zero's behind it.

Many other solar systems exist within this Universe, each exploring the theme that the solar system consciousness wishes to explore. The exploration of free choice extends to all souls, all consciousnesses, within this Universe. Each solar system is one consciousness, one soul, which has chosen to explore the possibilities contained within its own potential. Given the nature of our solar system, the structure here is a little different.

There is one Sun, one energy source. Then there were, originally, thirteen planets. Each of these were independent souls who chose to be within our solar system taking on a particular role. The Sun provided a 'physical' source of energy, the light and power to feed the life that was to, hopefully, develop. Each planet was to design and nurture their own forms of life and take their source of nourishment from the Sun.

Thirteen planets, thirteen forms of expression and thirteen forms of development. Thirteen attempts at life.

All were successful.

Thirteen planets each nurturing their own ideas and expressions of what physical life should look like. Each created their own form of a primary, conscious being, their own equivalent of a human being. Some were closer to fish forms, some were closer to reptiles and some were more like insects. What each had in common was that they were capable of containing the whole of the soul of those who also wanted to take part in this experiment of the physical.

So, we have three levels of existence coming together to form one whole. A consciousness on a solar system level, the Sun. Thirteen individual souls, each creating a planet and its forms of life. Then there were the souls who would take on the form of the individuals of the primary life forms on each planet.

It worked.

Each of the thirteen planets developed a primary life form and a huge diversity of other life in their plants and animals. The concept of 'physical' life proved to be the most abundant form within this Universe. The potential for diversity of life was found to be limitless. The joy of this discovery created ripples throughout this and other Universes.

Here was the answer to life, here were all of the answers to all of the Creator's questions. Physical life. Within the realms of the physical all possibilities can exist. All freedoms of expression can find form as nowhere else. The way in which the potential of any Universe can be explored is through the expression of life within the physical realms.

This is what makes our Universe so special, what makes our solar system so special. We found a way of answering any question the Creator might ask. All of the other Universes have only found part of an answer. What we achieved within this universe was the answer to all of the questions that have ever been asked.

That was our beginning.

The time on Atlantis really was the 'Garden of Eden', a place where humanity, all of the animals, all of the Faerie and the Sidhé (pronounced Shee) with all of their amazing plant creations lived in total harmony and peace.

All living things communicated openly, freely and psychically. There was no need for clothes as we were totally in tune with the environment. There was no need for permanent shelters as all that was needed were caves or tree nests such as those made by chimpanzees. Complete attunement with and between all living things. Our life expectancy was around fifteen hundred years and when we 'died' we could observe the work on Earth and communicate with those who were still physical. We did not use sexual reproduction at that time, so being reborn into human form just involved cloaking the soul in the matter of the Earth itself to give us full adult bodies. Nobody suffered any kind of illness and everybody could choose their lives and their interactions with any living thing. This was Earth, this was Atlantis, paradise made physical and all benefited and the Universe came to wonder.

Just when we began to change, nobody really knows as the process of change was very, very gradual and then not noticed until too late. It has taken us seventy five thousand years to find the answer to what brought about our problems and how to overcome them.

With hindsight, the story can be told.

The problems began with the slowing of the higher brain functions. This is to do with our abilities to psychically communicate with other people and other living things on the planet. We, ever so slowly, began to notice that it was increasingly difficult to communicate in this way. All souls within the Universe communicate by psychic means and so, to those who were on Atlantis, this form of communication was natural. As we began to, apparently, slow down, losses to this function were the first to be noticed. It was a little like television reception. Normally, the reception and transmission was perfectly clear but 'interference' began to be noticed. Images and messages began to become a little 'fuzzy' around the edges and then they gradually slowed so that an act of extreme concentration was required to pass even the simplest messages. This slowing took place over several hundred years; this is why it took so long to notice.

Other things then began to happen. Our communication with wild, predatory animals was instantaneous but this began to slow and so we began to feel threatened by their presence, particularly at night. We began to build shelters, communal sleeping places where a guard could be kept to ensure that no predators could approach unnoticed. The beginnings of the loss of trust between man and animals.

This loss of trust began to build fear amongst the human population, very subtly at first but also insidious, like a drip feed into the sub-conscious. Never before had this kind of fear and mistrust ever been experienced. We began to shrink inwards, away from the world. Daytime was fine but night time began to hold fear for us. Protection became an issue whereas it had never been before. As fear began to take hold, we also began to close inwards into ourselves and we began to argue. Factions began to form. Aggression began to show up for the first time. How? We lived on a world of perfect harmony. For fifteen thousand years we had lived in harmony with all living things, now we had begun to develop fear for other living things and aggression towards each other.

Then things really deteriorated.

Atlantis was a place where experimentation was actively encouraged and most took advantage of this opportunity to explore the possibilities that our new found paradise had to offer. The human body proved to be very adaptable to physical variations and changes.

The genetic accelerator 'chips' developed to accelerate Cro Magnon man into Homo Sapien Sapien could be reprogrammed to make almost any desired adaption to the human body.

For example, in taking seriously our role of responsibility for animal types, some chose to reflect their wish to work with a particular animal group consciousness by making modifications to their own skin. This was achieved by programming one of these genetic chips and inserting the chip into the equivalent of the heart chakra; we had no chakras at this time as the whole soul was in the body. Within three months of the chip's insertion, the body's skin would have changed to whatever it was designed to be: tiger, leopard, crocodile, Ibis, cat, all were possible and many people made modifications in this way. You only have to look at the later Egyptian 'gods' to see how effective these changes could be. The South American 'god' Quetzelcoatle for example, was someone who was very tall with long white hair that used one of these chips to take on the skin patterns of the diamond-backed rattlesnake and became 'The Plumed Serpent' that the name means.

Huge experimentation took place leading to more and more bizarre forms and mixes. When this mixing of animal and human characteristics together with a wish for experiment-ation was then met with the drop in consciousness levels, there began a process of some taking others to experiment on and the downward spiral accelerated.

The worst excesses of these experiments went to live in a network of catacombs three miles beneath the Earth's surface and these were only finally cleared out in 2002. It was these experimental excesses which led to many legends around the world of strange 'beasts and beings' emerging from deep cave systems and abducting women and animals and then disappearing again into the deep caves. Some of these kinds of abductions were reported up until at least 1995.

Hitler made notes in his diaries about being visited by beings that lived in deep catacombs beneath the Earth. He was so frightened by these visits that it led to some of his excesses but mainly to the beginnings of what has become known as

'Eugenics', the development of the physical into the 'perfect' Arian race of humans.

The original thoughts behind the Frankenstein story were memories of this time on Atlantis.

Ultimately, by general consensus, these experiments were stopped and Atlantis cleansed of those who carried out the worst excesses of experimentation.

Atlantis calmed and the wanting for experimentation waned. What we began to do was to start to look at why we were losing the highest aspects of ourselves, but no answer was found. There appeared to be no way of answering this particular question. Was it within the process of becoming physical? Was there something within 'physical' tissue that created a block on the soul's energies? Was there something on the planet that created too much change within the soul? Ultimately, our search for answers was cut short.

The abundance of life on Earth makes it the perfect place for providing templates for life on other worlds. These templates are the genetic, but primarily the energetic, 'blueprints' for life.

The modifications made to a bacterial life form destined for another world somehow were released on to the Earth's surface. Just how is lost in the mists of time, not even the Akashic records the process. It was not noticed at first and so its introduction into human life was slow to develop. It was, after all, a natural life form of this planet and there are many thousands of bacterial forms with which we share our world. Everything we touch carries some kind of bacteria. Most of these bacterial forms are harmless; they carry out work on the planet that helps everything else exist. This one was different.

Whilst it had been modified for life on another world, it carried the energy 'signature' of the Earth and so was almost impossible to detect beyond the normal bacterial background forms.

The function of this particular bacteria was to convert oxygen to hydrogen. Many bacterial forms on Earth carry out this kind of gas exchange function. However, this bacteria had been modified for life on another planet where life was just developing and so its gas-changing capabilities needed to be extremely strong. Some of the scientific models for early life on Earth are not too far wrong in terms of the caustic and poisonous atmosphere that was originally here. These stages in early Earth development were necessary in order to establish a basic foundation from which life could emerge. Most of the initial work on Earth to establish a suitable atmosphere for life was accomplished by altering bacteria from other worlds and introducing them here to establish a similar gas exchange process.

The modifications made to an Earth bacteria were to perform a similar task on a newly emerging world in another galaxy, a repayment of a favour, if you like. The problem arose when the modified form of the bacteria somehow became released on Earth.

This was no ordinary bacteria. On the other world, its function was perfectly balanced to how the planet needed to alter its atmospheric mix. On Earth, it proved deadly and unstoppable.

The nearest analogy is the current experiments carried out to genetically modify food plants and animals, another Atlantean memory trying to resolve itself. What genetic modification is doing is to take naturally occurring organisms and mix them with ones that are also naturally occurring. The mix, however, is between organisms that could not naturally cross in nature. Fish and tomatoes cannot possibly breed naturally with each other. There are also other parallels with Atlantean experimentation ongoing at this moment. Stem cell research, human cloning, gene therapy, all are heading us back to distant memories that have their echoes seventy thousand years ago. The memories of that time must be cleansed, but in doing so we are in danger of repeating the same mistakes with the same possible outcomes.

The accidental release of the modified bacteria on Atlantis had a devastating effect. There are no natural reasons to mix bacterial functions in this way – not for Earth. What this bacteria had the capability of doing was to destroy all life on Earth. If all of the oxygen in the body is converted to hydrogen, all that is left is a collection of minerals, not unlike salt. The free release of these modified bacteria on to the Earth had repercussions that had the potential to destroy all life. The same as GM organisms.

Ultimately, many tried to find a solution to dealing with this bacteria, all failed.

We, collectively, had two problems that appeared to be unsolvable. The loss of higher psychic functions of the soul and the arrival of a bacteria which had the potential to destroy all of the life on the planet.

Ultimately, there was only one answer – destroy the continent. We needed to contain the bacteria within Atlantis before it spread to other parts of the planet and we also needed to help humanity leave Earth before our loss of soul functions led us to depths we did not even begin to understand or wish to explore at that time.

The Mid Atlantic Trench was opened and the resulting volcanoes sank the continent into the Earth's magma core. Collective decisions, collective actions. Atlantis was sunk very deliberately into oblivion. Nothing could remain that could infect Earth, all was destroyed – deliberately and with collective choice. All knew what was proposed and all knew the outcome. Nothing could remain of Atlantis as that might reinfect the Earth with bacteria.

A partial solution, but not the answer to our original problems of loss of soul function. That still needed to be resolved.

Chapter Two

New Beginnings

With Atlantis destroyed, the vast number of souls who had come to Earth returned to their original homes, their place of soul origin. This was mainly to the six regions of the Universe where those who do not have any physical form originate. However, many thousands of souls from the semi-physical races elected to stay on Earth and the surrounding solar system, in order to put their combined skills to work on repairing the damage resulting from the sinking of a continent.

Those who remained in physical, human, form constructed for themselves vast underground refuges in several locations on the planet. Beneath the Sphinx in Egypt is a huge network of tunnels and chambers - even a fresh water lake up to 2 km across. In South America, there is a tunnel network of similar proportions to Egypt linking all of the ancient pyramid sites together extending over ten thousand kilometres with fresh water lakes built in several locations. In Britain, there are similar chambers built under Salisbury plain in Wiltshire. Although not of the expanse of the Egyptian or South American refuges, they do extend for several hundred kilometres.

Many of the semi physical individuals also made use of the Atlantean genetic "chips" to alter their physical bodies to give them protection or survival tools to help them survive the massive weather changes, volcanic eruptions and earthquakes that were ravaging the planet's surface.

These genetic changes to the human form were usually based on animal genetic characteristics. Many, for example, took on snake digestive systems. This allowed them to control the need for any kind of food for very long periods as snakes can take up to three months to digest a single meal. Some took on protective 'shells' such as those found with limpets. By having a very hard outside shell, they could curl up inside of it to protect themselves from extreme weather or rock falls.

There were those who used gecko genes, allowing them to be self-repairing of any injury as well as an ability to store fat in many regions of the body that could be used to feed themselves in times of starvation.

Some took to being able to communicate and breathe on land as well as living and breathing under water. This led to the creation of "mermaids". Many variations on these types of survival tools were made use of, all allowing the individual to survive on Earth during this period of reconstruction.

The damage caused to the Earth was immense.

Atlantis was a continent that stretched from the Atlantic side of Ireland, diagonally across the Atlantic as far as the Caribbean basin. In land mass terms, we are looking at a continent about the same area as South America.

The way in which 'we' dealt with the problems on Atlantis was to create a fissure in the Earth's crust stretching from The North Pole to the Southern Ocean. The original fissure surrounded the whole continent, engulfing Atlantis in volcanic magma and dragged the continent back into the Earth's core. With the continent sunk, the surrounding volcanic chains collapsed and, like a zip fastener closing, the middle of the Atlantic sea floor closed leaving the Mid Atlantic Ridge.

As a result of this change to the planet's surface, many other changes occurred.

The Mediterranean Sea was formed from a low-lying swamp. The Alp Mountains were formed from low foothills. The Himalayas were forced to their new heights from an already existing mountain range. The African Great Rift Valley was formed by two continents tearing themselves apart as the crust shifted into its new position. A large landmass between Japan and Australia sank.

These crustal shifts led to the current scientific thinking that 'Plate Tectonic' theory is how landmasses are in their current position. The land masses of the Earth have always been in positions relative to their current positions, the Earth has just expanded and contracted relative to mass consciousness energies rather than there being continental migration. With the destruction of Atlantis, however, the Earth's crust did shift and the continents found themselves in their current positions.

Most importantly, the Earth's axis shifted by six degrees.

When the Solar system came into existence, all of its thirteen planets were in perfect alignment with each other. All orbited around the Sun's equatorial axis. As the other four planets left, great changes occurred throughout the solar system and the life it supported. Almost all of the planets lost their life forms and they went into a state of stasis. The Earth just survived, with a great deal of help. All of the other planets moved into a state of imbalance and their orbits became less than perfect. But Earth survived with a vertical axis, until we removed Atlantis.

Atlantis was chosen because its position on the planet's surface gave it the average of all of the planet's climate options. Everything was possible on Atlantis because of its relative position.

Generally, the climate at the time of Atlantis was divided into two. The Southern Hemisphere had the South Pole and all of the turmoil of the Southern Oceans. The equatorial regions were then more or less as they are now but the Northern Hemisphere was sub tropical. The North Pole did not exist; it was a temperate region where tree ferns grew. The Northern Hemisphere did not have winters. By the planet's axis shifting, a wobble began within its orbit. The North Pole froze bringing with it all of the implications for the life that inhabited the northern half of the planet.

This is the reason why so many souls remained on Earth following the destruction, to help all of the life in the Northern Hemisphere to survive the change.

Those who originate on the star system we know as NGC 584 are master geneticists. They have worked with all of the life on Earth ever since it was first introduced twenty five million years ago. Several of the other races have worked with the NGC over many thousands of years and have developed similar skills and knowledge to the NGC.

All of the semi-physical races have a name for their 'home' star system and we have generally adopted these names as well. The Sirians called their home star system Sirius and the Pleiadeans called theirs the Pleiades. The NGC 584 home world, though, does not translate into anything that the human voice box can pronounce. The name the NGC have given to themselves has about twenty-five syllables with letters that have no counterpart in any human language. As a psychic thought form it is fine but as a spoken word, it cannot be pronounced. However, it is quite strange that we have not invented a name for them as they have been the one race who have helped develop and nurture all life on Earth from its very beginnings.

NGC 584 is a number from a star system numbering method that is used by astronomers. It stands for New General Catalogue (of stars) number 584 in the listing system, nothing more than that. But the NGC's impact on Earth, as their impact on all life on other worlds, deserves far greater recognition than is currently understood.

NGC 584 is located within the arc of the seven stars of the Pleiadean system, but very much more distant than the Pleiades are. Like our solar system, there are a number of planets orbiting a central sun. The difference between their star system and ours is that the NGC home world is located roughly in the position of Pluto within our solar system. This means that the energy from their very distant sun does not warm the planet's surface to any great extent and the surface temperature is close to what we on Earth would call absolute zero, minus 273 degrees centigrade.

To us, this seems impossible. How can life exist at temperatures that would freeze us so solid that we would shatter into millions of pieces if struck? But, for these beings, they are perfectly adapted to the conditions on their own world. The one big advantage that these temperatures give these people is that they are the perfect conditions for storing any genetic material from anywhere within this Universe. The NGC hold and store the genetic and energetic 'blueprints' of all life that has ever existed anywhere within this Universe and are capable of designing and constructing any life form that any planetary consciousness requires.

This is an awesome capability, potential and responsibility. They hold all of the secrets of life but they also act with immense integrity. They do not have any agenda other than to construct the 'physical' tissues around the energy structures that a planet provides. It is the planet that provides the 'soul' energy necessary to build a new life, be that plant or animal, but it is the NGC who give that 'soul concept' its required form.

The higher life forms, such as the consciousness that makes up each individual, be that 'Angel', Pleiadean, NGC or Sirian etc, come directly from the Creator but the life forms that inhabit each planet, plant or animal, is 'created' by the planet itself. It is at the request of the planet's own consciousness that the NGC act and put 'flesh on the bones' of the planet's ideas.

This is a difficult concept for us humans to come to terms with. There are many levels to the act of creation of a form of life. The Creator ultimately creates all life. However, each Creator-created soul is capable of their own acts of creation, from the humblest single cell organism up to the massive creationary potential of a galaxy. All create using the inherent energy, the inherent 'soul force', to bring about new life whether that is a copy of themselves or a new form of plant or planet, that potential for creation exists in all life.

Our Universe, our 'thought bubble' was the first ever to be created and was imbued with the energies that relate to absolute freedom of choice. Every soul that exists within this Universe has an absolute freedom of choice over their actions. In other words, there is no direction, there is no interference within the choices we, as created souls, make. Each is responsible for their own actions and each must take responsibility for their own actions. The Creator does not direct nor does 'It' interfere. The Creator has 'given' choice to all that there is within this Universe - why should it further interfere?

The nearest analogy is in baking a cake. You mix together all of the ingredients and pour the mixture into a mould. Then, you place the mould into the oven and allow it to 'cook'. You do not open the oven door every two seconds and rearrange the currants; you allow the ingredients to work it out for themselves.

This is the essence of free choice. We do as we choose. We act within the abundance of energies within this Universe and we choose to take actions, without interference and without direction from any source.

'God' does not dictate. 'God' does not direct. 'We' choose.

For many, their choice was to remain on the Earth and help it survive the damage we had done to it by destroying the continent of Atlantis.

The NGC, in particular, together with the Sirians and the Pleiadeans helped the Earth to rebalance and rebuild.

Many, many changes and readjustments were required.

The largest, and most urgent problem was the climate in the Northern Hemisphere and the impact on the life that lived there.

The planet's axis had always been vertical. The axis now took on a 'shift' of about six degrees. This axis shift meant that the North Pole froze and, with it, most of the Northern Hemisphere, creating the last Ice Age, 65 000 years ago. Every life form that inhabited the Northern Hemisphere had to change. Before the destruction, there was abundance and semi-tropical weather conditions. Life was abundant and plentiful. Suddenly, there were winters. Not only winters but the total freezing of all life, the best conditions for the NGC to work under.

Every life-form, from the tiniest bacteria to the largest mammoth, had enjoyed a life of abundance every day. That all now changed.

The six-degree axis shift was not sustainable as the planet would 'wobble' itself to destruction and so was corrected to four degrees - not desirable but sustainable. The life that depended on the Earth, though, required considerably more help.

Every life form needed to be helped to survive the change. A situation unprecedented in the history of any planet. Those who had the energetic and genetic strength to survive this level of change were helped to do so. Many were lost. Many new life forms had to be created to fill the voids. This was a work of momentous proportions.

The planet itself also needed a great deal of help. Six degrees of axis shift was unsustainable as far as the planet's own consciousness was concerned. The resulting wobble was self-destructive and needed to be corrected to at least four degrees. At four degrees, stability was possible but it would lead to harsh winters whereas none were present before, but at least the planet would survive. We were that close to destruction.

Other factors were the way in which the Earth's crust needed to move in order to compensate.

The Alps did not exist 65,000 years ago. The shift in the structure of the Atlantic landmass meant that the country of France was forced into Switzerland, raising land levels alarmingly. The whole of the Atlantic basin shifted back and forth as the new mid-Atlantic trench found its position in the ocean floor. Huge deposits of sediment were dumped on both the American shoreline and the French and Portuguese. These deposits have led to a great many scientific misunderstandings about continental drift. Magnetic pole positions underwent massive fluctuations until they finally settled.

The continent of India slammed into the Tibetan plateau that had been a low-lying plain until then, raising the Himalayas to their dizzy heights and pushing the Tibetan plains to some of the highest on the planet. The Great Rift Valley in Africa was formed by the tearing apart of a great landmass.

Norway became separated from the rest of the Scandinavian landmass and many of the fjords were formed. Denmark almost became an island instead of being attached to Germany. Iceland did become an island, totally detached from Greenland.

The list is endless. The changes to the planet's surface landmasses were beyond expectations and life almost ceased. Those who remained to work with these problems either took to the depths of the Earth or built themselves their own shelters, as described earlier. Nothing on Earth remained as it was at the time of Atlantis – nothing. All changed in some way. Some subtly, most devastatingly so. Everything needed to be rebuilt in some way and this work took 40 000 years.

Twenty-five thousand years ago the Earth finally began to settle and its new or modified life forms were established and flourishing. The Earth had a new axis angle of four degrees off the vertical and the season of winter in the Northern Hemisphere was firmly established. Stability was more or less reachieved. Never again would an Ice Age be required for the NGC to work unhindered but we would see some rebalancing by the Earth itself in the form of volcanoes or the occasional very harsh winters up until the mid 1800's.

Everything was allowed to settle – to find a new balance for the next five thousand years.

One of the primary 'what ifs' of this Universe is to explore if the possibility of 'physical' life, in the form of humanity, could exist.

The attempt on Atlantis had led to a major success but also to a major failure. Whilst the possibility of success appeared feasible, the practice was a long way from proof. Nobody knew why Atlantis had failed. The removal of the bacterial problem might have been necessary to save the Earth but humans had begun to experience problems long before the bacteria proved to be any kind of a threat.

Many, many questions were asked of all of the souls inhabiting this Universe. All have absolute free choice within the matter of human life and an opinion was needed from the whole Universal soul. Do we try again?

The energy resources required to fulfil the Creator's wish for experimentation on a human level were enormous. Many other potential 'projects', potential choices, had to be put on hold whilst Atlantis was in existence. Did we continue to drain Universal resources for a project that, apparently, had too many problems that were not understood?

Obviously, it was considered important enough to try to find the answers otherwise we would not exist.

Twenty thousand years ago, we began again.

The time spans here seem impossibly long to our human perceptions. We knew the Earth had reached its balance 25,000 years ago and yet it took 5,000 years before we reached a decision.

5,000 years to us is about 500 years to the semi-physical races but about 5 years to the non-physical races. Given that it was intended that the non-physical races were the souls to take part in this human experiment, it was their choices that were paramount.

Twenty thousand years ago, a 'delegation' comprised of all of the races connected with the Earth came to visit. They communicated with every living organism on this planet as well as the planet itself and presented their proposals for a new approach.

The final agreement was this:

Six regions of the planet were to be designated 'experimental'. All life that could possibly be affected by our experimentation was moved, with its agreement and choice, to other regions of the planet which were to be considered 'out of bounds' by those who were to run the new experiment. This is the principal reason behind human 'migration' at this time. Nothing to do with climate change or movement 'out of Africa', just agreed clearances for a new beginning.

These six regions were:

South America - particularly Mexico, Guatemala and Belize. Although the continent was located much further out into the Pacific at the time of Atlantis, it shifted into its current location on 'the destruction'.

Mesopotamia - that which is now Southern Turkey, Syria, part of Iran and Northern Iraq, down to the Persian Gulf.

Egypt - most of the Red Sea coastline and parts of Ethiopia.

Northern Europe - Britain, Ireland and Northern France.

Tibet - the whole of the newly raised Tibetan Plateau.

Southern Greece - this was a region that stretched from Athene to Crete but was later partly destroyed by volcanic activity.

The first job was to connect all of the new energy patterns that were required for the task in hand.

The primary planetary energy intake point at Silbury Hill in Wiltshire was enhanced to feed the whole planet. A massive new energy 'grid', that which have become known as 'ley lines' to most people, connected all regions of the planet.

Into precise locations new 'gateways' were constructed. These gateways allowed the new arrivals to travel at will across the planet but only to the specific agreed locations of the six sites.

In Mexico at Teotehuacan.

In Mesopotamia close to modern day Esfahan in Iran.

In Egypt where the Sphinx is located.

In Britain at Stonehenge.

In Tibet near Garyarsa.

In Southern Greece the land on which the 'gate' stood is now underwater.

Once all of these energy rearrangements were completed, the first of those who were to try and find the answers began to arrive. In total, two thousand one hundred and fifty arrived at this stage scattered amongst all six sites. They entered through the solar system gateway of Orion and, once on Earth, began to condense their energies into the body form developed on Atlantis. This is a process known as Adult Birth and was the only method of taking on human form for the next few thousand years until sexual reproduction and birth were adopted. This method of arrival is the origin of the story of Adam and Eve.

Humans were once again present on the Earth.

Chapter Three

The Road to Answers

The biggest problem of all was where to begin.

Those of the semi-physical races who had remained on Earth to repair the damage had themselves experienced the loss of higher consciousness functions that had been experienced on Atlantis but had no clues as to why the problem occurred. Their only way of 'healing' themselves had been to leave the planet for a short while in order to recuperate. Once they returned, the problems would gradually begin again.

Everything on every level was investigated. The Earth now had more or less a stable pattern of life and all of this life resonated at energy frequencies compatible with 'physical' existence. Eventually it was decided that the problem was a fundamental part of being 'physical', but, in order for the Creator's wish to be fully investigated, a way of overcoming the problem needed to be found.

Those who had remained on Earth found that the problems began after about 200 years on the planet. Given that the average life span on Atlantis was about 1,500 years, this was far too short a time to be acceptable and the idea of having to leave the body every 200 years did not seem to be a reasonable solution as 200 years was considered too short a time period for the individual to fulfil their choices for that lifetime.

In order to remain on the planet's surface for longer periods than this, a programme of buildings was begun that were designed to overcome the loss of consciousness problems.

The Sphinx had already been built by those who remained on Earth to carry out the repair work. The Sphinx originally had the face of a lion. This idea was simply to deter the pre-human population from entering the cave systems built under it, but also as a marker for those travelling through the Orion Gate to visit Earth to monitor progress. The lion's face was changed many centuries later by a late-dynasty Pharaoh.

The earliest of these buildings were the seven major pyramids of Egypt. Egypt was chosen to be the first to experiment with these structures as, although the climate was sub-tropical at the time, the underlying soil structure contained a high proportion of mica, a substance that will not allow energy to pass through it. This was necessary in order to prevent the energy flow concentrated here from affecting the Earth's own energy fields. By the time the pyramids were complete, the climate had already begun to dry and the region was turning into its current desert state.

An overall plan of this pyramid complex shows that the layout mirrored precisely the seven principal stars of Orion. Whilst the three pyramids of 'Orion's Belt' are the ones that have become famous in recent times, all seven of the original pyramids were a fundamental part of the whole interactive structure. All seven collected and focussed energy into the central one of the 'belt', the one that stands the closest to the Sphinx. This central pyramid was further enhanced in its energy-focussing capabilities by being totally clad in a thin layer of gold and with massive crystal structures, like antennae, located on the four base corners, mid-way up the slopes and the main one, fifteen foot tall (5 metres), on top of the pyramidion.

Many buildings and other structures have been added to this complex over the centuries by numerous Pharaohs and priests but the seven pyramids and the Sphinx were the first structures built by humans on the face of the planet (the ones built in the latter years of Atlantis were obviously destroyed along with the continent).

These pyramids were constructed by psychic means. Collectively, all of those in Egypt came together and, by focussing their thoughts, forced the thought through solid rock, perfectly forming block shapes. Once these blocks were formed and shaped, they were lifted and positioned, again by collective thought. This is another example of one of the higher consciousness functions we have lost, the ability to form and use thoughts to work in these kinds of ways. Collectively, we could literally move mountains by thought alone.

Within all of these pyramids a number of chambers were constructed. These chambers were never intended to be used as 'tombs' and they never have been. The purpose of the chambers were points at which various energies could be focussed and then made use of by someone standing or lying within the chamber. At first, only the central, so called King's Chamber, was necessary to be used in this way.

The idea was that by entering this chamber, the focus of energy was sufficient to re-merge the aspects of the higher consciousness that were being lost. As the centuries progressed, however, other chambers in other pyramids also needed to be used to have the same effect. We have fallen so far from these states of consciousness that we do not now even remember what these structures were designed to create, let alone know how to use them.

Their function was this: each pyramid gathered together certain energy frequency ranges which were focussed into the main chamber. By visiting each pyramid in turn, it was possible to gather sufficient energy and knowledge to know how to use the central pyramid chamber and regain the whole consciousness ability.

Each chamber in each pyramid was assigned a 'name'. By speaking – pronouncing - this name correctly, the sounds generated 'standing wave' structures that resonated with the stones of the chamber. Then knowledge, and particular energy patterns, were released which enhanced the speaker. These are the actual 'Keys of Enoch', sound sequences which unlock doorways in the soul and allow in the knowledge of how to regain what we once were.

Eventually, the loss of consciousness functions became so great that we even lost the knowledge of the use of these teaching pyramids and certain people were designated to remember the 'Key' sequences. These 'Key' keepers led directly to the formation of a 'priesthood' type society where it was necessary to undergo initiation in order to learn the use and sequences of the 'Keys'. Over time, all of this knowledge was lost and man-made 'religions' have taken its place leading to a great loss of knowledge and freedom of thought.

The Egyptian structures had proven themselves to be very successful in their intended use but it was also found that a complex of this nature was not necessarily required.

In South America, a single pyramid at Teotehuacan was capable of doing the same job. In Tibet, another single pyramid was built but that was partly destroyed by earthquake 4,000 years ago and the site was taken over as a Buddhist temple. In Esfahan in Mesopotamia, a full pyramid was built but was later partly demolished and truncated for use by another man-made religion now long gone. In Greece, this pyramid was lost in the earthquake that sank all of the land.

The British site and structures were a little different.

Salisbury Plain was fully wooded at this time and so 'hiding' energy points and the entrance to the underground chamber system from the local inhabitants was fairly straightforward. Silbury Hill did not exist as a hill but was a clearing in the woods. Silbury was the primary energy intake point for Atlantis and, whilst it now switched roles to feeding the whole planet, building structures to protect the surrounding Earth energies were unnecessary. The 'hill' was built some time later to enhance specific energy requirements.

The entrance to the underground chambers built as shelters during the reconstruction works are located under West Kennet Long Barrow. The Barrow structure has nothing to do with these times; it was a much later addition. West Kennet was, and remains, the site of the most powerful upwelling of the Earth's own consciousness energy. This energy has nothing to do with the 'Ley Line' network; those are energy conduits through which the energy required to sustain human life travel.

The closeness to the Earth's own consciousness is the reason why Silbury was chosen as the energies directed at that point could also be made use of by the planet. The site for the 'gate' at Stonehenge was located for similar reasons and why it did not need to be 'insulated' from the surrounding land.

Development at Stonehenge followed similar lines to that of the Egyptian Pyramids in that it was only the energies of Stonehenge that were initially required and no enclosures were originally built. It was only as we began to lose our higher functions that the stone circle was constructed as a 'memory' structure.

As we further deteriorated, construction was begun on the stone circles at Avebury. The original intention of the six circles followed a similar concept to the six 'secondary' pyramids in Egypt. In other words the stones that make up the circles at Avebury are imprinted with the knowledge of how to use the gateway and consciousness enhancer that is Stonehenge.

To 'power up' the Avebury circles Silbury Hill was built. The energies entering Silbury travel directly into the ley line grid and into West Kennet. Silbury Hill is constructed in such a way that it acts like a giant 'battery', accumulating energy into the structure of the hill until it is required for use.

The use of the Avebury stones is similar to that of using all seven pyramids in Egypt. The 'initiate' would climb to the top of Silbury Hill and receive a huge boost to their energies. Using these extra energies, together with sound 'keys', the knowledge recorded within the stones could be unlocked. Once they had completed the rounds of all of the, originally, six stone circles, the initiate would know how to make full use of the Stonehenge energies.

Whilst Silbury still maintains its role as a primary energy intake point, the stones at Avebury have lost their secrets. The Christian Church began wholesale and deliberate destruction of the site in the 1700's. More recently, the primary ley lines, Michael and Mary, have also 'left' Avebury. The whole site has been totally disrupted over the years not only by the church but also by those who have 'played' with the energies without full knowledge of what they were doing. The Michael line has moved North to the middle of Exmoor whilst the Mary line has moved South through Silbury. They do not re-meet until they cross on the edge of Bodmin Moor in Cornwall. Avebury does have a new energy structure to it, such an important site will survive no matter what. This new energy is taking the form of a huge vortex under the remaining circles. Stonehenge is now fully operational again for those who have the knowledge of how to use it.

Once we had arrived at the point where the 'Key Keepers' became necessary, we realised that we were having major problems.

Yet again, the question arose of was it actually possible for humans to exist?

The Earth was prepared to continue, but was anyone else?

Another consensus was taken throughout the Universe about these questions.

The overwhelming response was that the question of human 'physical' life was a direct request from the Creator. This question was part of the fundamental energy structure of this Universe. If we abandoned the 'experiment' at this point with the problems left unanswered, the Universe would have to collapse back in on itself and, possibly, begin again. It was Universally felt that we should continue until, at least, we had found the answer.

By now, the new population had begun to 'mingle' with the possible human forms developed by the Earth and this was producing a new stage of development. It was possible to produce a complete human being, one that fitted into the Atlantis Template, but the result was not permanent.

As each generation developed, the 'human' problem became more pronounced. Life spans were dropping to about 800 years, maximum, instead of the original 1500 years and the dependency on the 'Key Keepers' was growing. New ways needed to be developed in order to help everyone understand who they were and what their purpose was.

The first idea was to develop 'pictograms' or hieroglyphs as the archaeologists call them. The original use of these 'pictures' was as reminders in the same way as the pyramids were intended to be but at one level lower. The pictograms were never intended to be 'read' as we would read a book. These were intended to be 'read' psychically as a reminder that we needed to seek out the 'Keys'. Even these began to need interpreters.

Eventually, about 12,000 years ago, a written and 'spoken' language needed to be developed as even some of our 'primary' psychic functions were beginning to be eroded.

The first 'language' to be developed operated on the level at which the brain and central nervous system functions. Primary 'physical' language. This was originally known as Hebrewa. It has become corrupted, made more 'physical', and adjusted to Hebrew. Hebrewa was a 'stem' language bringing about Runes and Ogham and from it sprang several cuniform languages. This development meant we were really starting to lose it.

Other developments were felt necessary at this time.

The Greeks began to record our history and put who and what we were into the new written forms.

The Mesopotamians began to map the body's workings and energy structures giving rise to the Ayurvedic traditions. These people first named the chakras, mapped the meridians and performed surgery. They also developed telescopes and microscopes to help them in their task.

The Celtic group in northern Europe used Ogham as a written form but, given their proximity to the primary energy sources, they held out against this reduction in the consciousness for much longer than the rest of the world and so developed the 'oral' recording techniques so beloved by the Celtic Bards.

By about 8,000 years ago, we were pretty much down to the level we are now.

We had become very physically dense, we had lost most of our psychic functions, we were down to two spirals to our DNA instead of the original thirteen and we had, by necessity, divided the soul into the 'higher self' and the 'physical self'. A huge loss of function, capability and potential. We were not even close to who we were, where we were or why we were here. It appeared as though all had been lost and we needed to abandon the 'experiment' before the soul became so degraded that we lost that as well.

Again, questions were asked. Again, answers were sought. Again, no answers were forthcoming. This was uncharted territory. Nobody throughout the whole of Creation had stood where we were then standing and nobody knew the way forward and nobody knew the reasons why.

We were, apparently, abandoned by the rest of the Universe to find our own way. This was not actually the case, but it took a long time to find out why.

Collectively, we took stock. We were nothing like we were when we arrived here. Most of the functions and abilities that made us 'us' were degraded, not lost, just generally not available. The whole soul was now in two parts, eleven thirteenths of our memory was lost (DNA), and we needed 'Key' keepers just to help us remember where we began to remember, let alone to remember at all and we needed language to communicate.

The Earth could not be abandoned. Too much had been put into where we were to walk away. The consciousness that is the Earth wanted to continue. What we needed to do was to find a way of meeting our task. Together, we made a collective decision.

We had become 'human', a part of the Earth. Our place, we realised, was here - whatever that meant. All of our trials and tribulations needed to be put to use, not walked away from. But where to go next?

Together, all of the billions of souls connected with Earth had to find a solution. We were clearly on our own.

What we came up with was 'Karma'. This is a Sanskrit word that means 'knowledge' in its original translation. What we proposed to do was to gain 'knowledge' of how to be human and regain our past potential, to rejoin the soul into one.

This process we began 7,000 years ago.

Each individual connected with earth was to live a series of lifetimes gathering knowledge of how to reconnect the soul, how to remember who and what we were. Collectively, we might actually arrive at the answer.

We entered into a contract with the earth. This contract stated very clearly that we would allow ourselves seven thousand years, at the outside, to find the answer. When all calendar adjustments are taken into account, the seven thousand year agreement finishes at the end of 2011.

The Earth is not recalculating nor is it renegotiating. That is all the time there is. 2011 or the experiment has failed.

All of the ancient calendars reflect this date. The Mayan, the Egyptian, the Tibetan, the Chinese etc calendars all have been misinterpreted to mean that human life ends in 2011. It is not the end of life they predict but the end of the time we allocated to ourselves to complete our chosen task.

Chapter Four

The Human Plan

This begins to all sound a little confusing.

On Atlantis we established a 'Human Template' which determined what was needed, in physical terms, for a soul to take on human form. This 'Template' was an energetic model of the human body. This was the basic pattern for the layout of the organs, the body's basic physical dimensions, sex (if one was chosen), soul energy requirements etc etc. The energetic structure of this template allowed for a lifespan of about 1,500 years. We had the full compliment of our genetic memories intact, thirteen strands to the DNA helix.

Once we had taken on human form we began to realise, after about 1,000 years or so, that there was subtle but noticeable slowing of the higher functions of our consciousness. However, there were so many changes and problems occurring in a situation that was entirely new that nobody noticed the extent of the problem until about 15,000 years into Atlantis's existence.

It really is not possible to describe the sum of the sensory awareness capabilities we had at that time and we can only just about imagine a world where we could translocate and bilocate or have full psychic communication. These were all abilities we had when we first arrived on Earth. As we became more accustomed to gravity and the feel of grass under our feet, very few people translocated as it was such a joy to walk everywhere.

Those who made use of the Atlantean genetic 'Chips' to take on animal characteristics further altered their perceptions and ways of being. Further problems were added as a number of souls were unsure of what to expect in taking on this new form and so had 'Linked' themselves together to share experiences and, particularly, any problems. Others had formed similar 'Links' on their arrival on Atlantis as they had experienced difficulties in becoming physical when they had never experienced physical density before.

These 'Links' are a soul to soul connection. It allowed those linked in this way to share experiences and emotions. Those who had asked for a link to be formed once they had arrived here were able to pass the energetic structure of their problems to another person who would then deal with the problems on their behalf – an ultimate form of healing. This is not along the lines of so-called 'soul mates'. Soul mates, in this sense, are just souls who have shared several lives together and their energies are very familiar. Soul to soul 'Links' are very different and are effectively permanent and are still causing major problems in this current lifetime.

Once we had destroyed Atlantis, the 'Human Template' was stored by the planetary consciousness for future use.

Those who remained on the Earth to help sort out the problems caused by the destruction noted that the loss of higher consciousness functions was more marked and now tended to occur after about two hundred years. The main cause for the difference in time frames, 1,000 years as opposed to 200 years, appeared to be caused by the shift in the Earth's axis from totally vertical to a four degree angle off the vertical.

This angle shift seemed to be generating unusual ripples in the Earth's energy patterns and the reduction in timeframe was put down to these ripples.

When we returned, 20,000 years ago, these ripples were still in place and were probably responsible for our encountering problems very rapidly.

Every attempt we made to overcome these losses of functions had failed and we were not really any closer to finding the source of the problem. Everyone on Earth at that time had their theories but none proved to be an answer. We were also far too busy trying to resolve the problems to devote much time to looking for the root cause.

It also appeared as though we had used up a huge amount of time, but in reality time is ultimately relative. Fifty years ago, one year 'felt' like it was one year long. More recently, particularly since 1996, we have felt that time is passing very much more quickly and one year 'feels' more like six months. This change in perception has arisen because of the shift in energy patterns and levels of consciousness of everyone on the planet. The higher the levels of consciousness we achieve the faster time relatively passes.

By the time we arrived at eight thousand years ago, we had apparently lost the fight. We had divided the soul into two and lost eleven thirteenths of our genetic memories and our average lifespan was down to about 120 years. In between lifetimes it was necessary to reconnect with the total soul and rejuvenate ourselves off the planet.

When we did return for a new human lifetime we found that whilst we could adopt the original 'Template' we could not sustain it for very many years and we then slipped into the divided situation we were becoming used to.

The Universe had also apparently abandoned us to whatever we made of the situation (see chapter five). The primary gateway to the rest of the Universe, through the constellation of Orion, had effectively been sealed and we could not leave the solar system. The other gateway, through the constellation of Draco, which led to the realms of the semi-physical races, had also become very restricted. We were effectively sealed into the solar system for reasons we were unaware of and we had no choice but to continue in the best ways we could.

Within this Universe, the way in which decisions are made is along the lines of a consensus. Each soul makes a personal decision on any given issue and then adds their 'vote' to everyone else's. Once this kind of vote has been taken, the majority view is usually enacted. Once the decision is made, all souls within the Universe take appropriate action, a truly Universal soul action.

Given we were shut off from the rest of the Universe, we had to take this kind of consensus action ourselves. This needed to be done by the whole, reunited soul of the individual. In other words, everyone had to leave their physical bodies, reunite with their higher selves for this problem to be fully discussed and a solution arrived at.

It was clearly not possible for everyone to leave the planet's surface at the same time as crops and animals needed to be tended so those who elected to stay agreed to accept the decision made by the whole. This act of leaving the Earth's surface has led to the scientific view that some kind of mass human extinction occurred seven and a half thousand years ago. It is true, but we just left to vote. The Earth, the Sidhé and several billion souls were present.

The decision was this: it was clear that we could not continue as we were, too many problems were being encountered that were becoming increasingly difficult to overcome. We could not leave the solar system and so had to find a solution by ourselves.

The problem was, clearly, being human on a planet that generated energy patterns to sustain physical life. What we needed to do was to become a part of those patterns in order to fully understand what underlay the problems we were experiencing. To this effect, we designed a new 'Human Template' which reflected what we had become – a soul divided into higher and physical aspects and a reduced genetic memory structure. This template was to be adopted as the 'temporary' human state until we found a way of reclaiming our original template. The Earth agreed to sustain us in this 'sub-human' state for a period of seven thousand years. If we did not achieve our goal by then, we would all have to leave the planet and return to our home regions of the Universe. The seven thousand year period was insisted upon otherwise the Earth would be too depleted to sustain the rest of the life that inhabited its surface.

For our part, we were to live a series of lifetimes using the new human template with the physical aspect of the soul living these lives under the direction of the higher aspect of the soul.

This knowledge-gathering process we have come to know as 'Karma', a Sanskrit word meaning 'knowledge'. Many have subsequently tried to turn this concept into something else, some kind of debt, but all we have been doing for the past seven thousand years is gathering knowledge of how to be human.

The experiences and knowledge gained would be stored by the 'higher self' which would design the experiences needed for each lifetime in such a way that maximised knowledge.

Everyone else would share the accumulated knowledge gained by each individual by placing it into a collective library, a collective 'record'. The word 'record' in Sanskrit is 'Akashic'. Sanskrit was used as it was the peoples in the Mesopotamia region who had developed this language whilst they were undertaking what we would call 'scientific studies' of the Earth and all of its life.

This 'Karmic' process was begun seven thousand years ago and was stopped in 1996. By then, we knew the answer. The seven thousand years allotted to our process of learning stops with the end of 2011. If we cannot fit into the original Atlantean human template by then, we must leave the Earth and return 'home'.

Karma: the word means different things to different people. To Buddhists, the word has been retranslated to mean 'debt'. What actions are taken in one life must be atoned for in the next. To Hindu, the word means punishment. Actions taken in another life are punished in this. To those who have embraced the so-called 'New Age Movement', it is an excuse to avoid responsibility for any action in this lifetime as you are trying to clear 'something' from the past.

None of these interpretations are correct.

The purpose of Karma was to learn - to learn how to be human on our 'physical' world. Nothing more, just knowledge gathering. Each lifetime's choice of learning experience was planned by the higher self. All we, the human bits, have done is to enact the wishes of the soul.

The basic idea was simple. If we followed the soul's directions we remained healthy and fit, if we strayed from our soul's chosen path, we became ill, eventually died and tried again. We were not blind within this process. Those who were the Mesopotamian 'group' had taken on a 'scientific' role. They had mapped the body and all of its energy patterns. The 'Chakras', a Sanskrit word meaning 'spinning wheel of light', were aspects of the total soul represented within the 'physical' aspects of the soul, the physical body.

Each chakra represented an aspect of the whole soul and related to specific aspects of personality and to specific organs of the body, all incorporated in the new 'template'. The 'Higher' aspects of the soul would 'talk' to us through the chakras to ensure that we followed its directions fully. If we strayed from our soul's path, we depleted the energies of a particular chakra and an illness arose. By recognising which area of our lives needed correcting, we could take appropriate action, rebalance the chakra and remove the symptoms of illness. Simple. Except: we began to slip even further from where we were seven thousand years ago and we forgot the chakras and their meaning. Illness became some kind of punishment or accident or something that 'needed to be overcome', a test. Wrong.

The process is very simple and to understand the chakras, and their messages, we just need to delve into our individual and collective memories. We have allowed ourselves to be misled by the 'Church' and by the medical profession into believing that the 'Church' can heal the soul and the medical profession can heal the body, we do not need to take any responsibility for either. Leave it to someone else and all will be well.

In previous lifetimes our ignorance of the soul's promptings was not a major problem. If we took actions that were against the soul's wishes, we paid the price through illness and eventually died leaving the soul to incorporate our failure into the next or subsequent lifetime.

We no longer have this luxury.

The years of the twentieth century were ones of immense turmoil on a global level. All of the 'difficult' bits of learning we had put off from all of our lifetimes needed to be resolved before we hit our 2011 deadline. Many of the illnesses that arose through the last century were ones never seen before. The more we fought against the soul, the stronger the message the soul gave us and the more complex the messages became.

As we begin our climb back to regaining our full consciousness the chakra messenger system is taking on a greater significance. The chakras have changed colours beyond recognition and the speed of the messages is becoming instantaneous. Nobody is immune from the chakra-based messages; no matter how far down the route of reintegration they have travelled.

This is a brief description of the chakras. If you want a full explanation, that is detailed in *Everything You Always Wanted To Know About Your Body But, So Far Nobody's Been Able To Tell You.*

All of the chakras take the form of a 'vortex', with the point of the spiral attached to the spine with the 'cone' opening away from the body. The chakras do not, and never did, take any other shape.

The First Chakra
This first chakra is located at the very base of the spine, at the tip of the coccyx. The point of the vortex spiral is attached to the coccyx and the spiral opens directly downwards in a line with the spine.

This chakra's primary function is to literally 'root' the soul to the planet. Its secondary function is to build the 'physical' tissues of the body. The first chakra contains all of the information of the human template and this template is imprinted on to the body cells as they develop in the womb giving the body its form and function.

This chakra becomes affected if we feel insecure in what we are doing. It relates to the skeleton, muscles and skin in general and to the urinary system in more specific ways.

The way in which the chakra works is, briefly, this. If we feel a little insecure in what we are doing or the situations we are faced with, the skin becomes affected, something along the lines of eczema. If we do nothing to correct our insecurity, the muscles begin to ache and complain. If we still do nothing to make ourselves feel more comfortable, the bones can become affected such as in conditions like osteoporosis. Osteoporosis has nothing to do with hormones - just long term insecurity.

The urinary system becomes affected if there is a situation which we have been trying to deal with but there are still aspects of the problem ongoing. Insecurities of this nature are what brings on incontinence, usually in the young or the elderly.

The Second Chakra

This is located where the spine meets the pelvis, at the top of the sacrum bone. There is a vortex connected on the spine that opens equally front and back. The illustration only shows the back aspect of the chakra for clarity.

The chakra has two functions. Its primary function is our creativity. Its secondary function is connected with our sexual relationships; these are sexual partners such as husband and wife.

It relates to the sexual reproduction organs, testes, prostate etc in men and the uterus, ovaries etc in women.

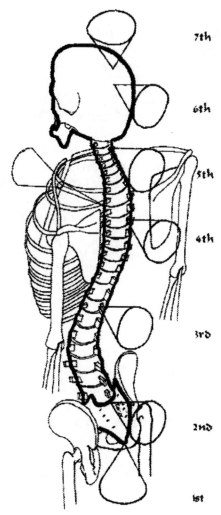

7th

6th

5th

4th

3rd

2nd

1st

The Seven Primary Chakras

Most problems arise with these organs when we are having problems with our partners. If we switch to the chakra's primary role and get back in touch with our creative side, these kinds of problems can be overcome. If we have 'structural' problems in this region such as lower back pain, pelvic or hip pain, it is because we are insecure within either our sexual relationship or within our creativity.

The Third Chakra

This is located in the middle spine, on a line just above the tummy button. This chakra's primary function is with personal power issues. Its secondary function deals with the emotions we express, or don't express, in these kinds of situations.

The connected organs are: the liver, the gall bladder, the pancreas, the spleen, the stomach and intestines.

The liver acts as a central processor for all of the emotions, distributing them to their appropriate organ. The liver, itself, deals with the 'big' emotions of guilt, jealousy and, in particular, fear.

The gall bladder deals with unexpressed anger.

The pancreas deals with the amount of force we should use in expressing ourselves but do not. For example, if we should have screamed and shouted in a situation but all we actually did was to mutter under our breath, all of the unexpressed 'force' of the emotion affects the pancreas.

The spleen deals with frustration, particularly frustration connected with unexpressed anger. On a physical level, one of its functions is to control the operation of the lower body lymphatic system. If we store too much frustration, the lymphatic blocks up and we end up with cellulite and lower body weight gain – this is why diets never work, the food we eat has nothing to do with weight.

The stomach and intestines deal with two ends of the emotional spectrum. The stomach with an immediate situation. For example, if we encounter an horrific car crash and do not have an appropriate emotional response, we throw up the stomach's contents. The large intestines, the colon, on the other hand, deals with long-term emotional storage. If we do not deal with the situations we encounter in life we store the emotions in the colon. If there are colon problems, it is possible to know which region of our lives we have stored emotions from as they will be stored in specific locations. The stomach can be thought of as the immediate situation but, as you travel through the intestinal tract, you travel back in time so that the rectum, in emotional terms, relates to birth. The rectum to the last bend of the descending colon, the Sigmoid colon, relates to childhood and the bend itself to teenage. As we then move back up the descending colon, the closer we get to the present. The small intestine is a processor for the emotional storage.

The Fourth Chakra

This chakra is located about where the heart is. It deals with the heart and blood circulation, the upper body lymphatic system through the thymus gland and the endocrine system (the body's hormone system, of which there are about 70 hormones).

Its primary function is the seat of communication between the soul and the physical body. In its communication function, the soul uses the hormones - a Greek word meaning 'messenger' - to communicate the fact that we have gone astray from the soul's primary wishes. Its secondary function is how we express love, either for the self or to others.

Health problems related to this chakra are usually to do with our expressions of love. If we are not good at expressing our love to others, the heart tends to become affected – usually a male problem, although women can 'harden their heart' to themselves giving them heart problems. If we are not good at expressing our love towards ourselves, the thymus and upper body lymphatic system becomes blocked. Women are usually not good at this form of self expression and the ultimate outcome of denial on this level is breast cancer.

The Fifth Chakra

This is located in the throat, just above the Adam's apple. Again, the chakra is located on the spine with equal vortices opening out front and back. This chakra deals with self expression at its primary level and communication and judgement as its secondary. The connected organs are the lungs and the thyroid.

The lungs are more about the expression aspect, literally getting things off our chest whilst the thyroid is more about how comfortable we feel in expressing ourselves. The thyroid also controls the body's calcium balance, particularly in the spine, so the thyroid is about how confident/secure we feel in expressing our ideas (in relation to the first chakra). The thyroid also controls the body's metabolism, how effectively we use oxygen within the body to metabolise our food. A slow, underactive thyroid, relates to someone who wants to look bigger than they actually feel inside. An overactive thyroid relates to someone who slims down so much that they hope they will disappear into the background.

The Sixth Chakra

This is located in the centre of the forehead, just above the bridge of the nose. Its primary function is the part of our consciousness that deals with our 'spirituality', our sense of soul. Its secondary function is our psychic vision. It is mainly connected to our primary senses.

The nose, as in do we want to smell? The ears, do we want to hear? The left eye, do we want to see? The lower brain and the central nervous system, do we want to sense? The pituitary gland: this is the controlling gland for the endocrine system, the soul's messengers - do we want to listen to the soul?

The Seventh Chakra

This is located at the very top of the head, in a direct line with the spine. The point of the vortex is connected to the top of the head and the vortex opens directly upwards. This chakra is our direct energetic connection to the non physical aspects of the soul, the so-called 'higher self'.

It is connected to the upper brain, our thought and wisdom. To the right eye, again, do we want to see what is happening around us? Through the right eye it connects to the pineal gland. This is a gland at the base of the brain that produces a hormone called melatonin. Melatonin has two functions within the body. Firstly, as light falls and is detected through the right eye, melatonin levels rise and it is time to go to sleep. Secondly, melatonin works with our psychic functions, this is why so many mediums and psychics prefer to work in the dark (high melatonin levels).

ME, or Chronic Fatigue Syndrome, is also caused by melatonin. If we have gone so far against the soul that we refuse to listen to any of its prompts, it switches on the melatonin production and all we can do is slow down until we sort out the mess we have made of our lives.

This is a very brief guide to the chakras but from it can be seen that we do have communication with the rest of the soul - we have just forgotten how to listen.

The colours of the chakras have, traditionally been, from bottom to top: red, orange, yellow, green, blue, violet and indigo. Not one single person has these colours to their chakras any longer. The last person to try to hold on to these colours died in 2002. We will discuss the new colours later.

Chapter Five

Some Added Complications

Ours is not the only Universe to exist. There are currently eleven in total. Each Universe has its own 'thought bubble', its own 'what if' to explore. Each Thought requires its own energy patterns, its own mix of frequencies to explore its originating purpose. Many of the frequencies contained within this Universe are totally incompatible with those of other Universes.

Time frames and time sequences can be a little complicated to explain fully in terms of how we can comprehend them and is often beyond this author how to explain them in the way the Akashic records them. Thousands of years to us are hundreds to the semi-physical races and decades to the non-physical races. To add to this, each region of space can have its own time zones which can mix and blend all of the time sequences into vortices that can be travelled in both directions – forwards or back in time which add loops and swirls into any kind of calculation.

However, three and a half million years ago, beings from another Universe found a way of entering ours. This three and a half million year time frame somehow relates to the Universe shutting out Earth eight thousand years ago. Strange stuff, time.

Regardless of time frame differences, our Universe was entered by beings from another Universe who brought with them their own energy structures that were totally incompatible with the energy structures of our Universe.

Like all of the individual consciousnesses in all of the universes, these beings were humanoid in form but they also had a reptilian appearance. They were semi-physical in structure and the Universe has come to call them "The Fourteenth Faction".

Their apparent purpose in coming here was to strip this Universe of as many of its resources as they could in order to maintain a position within their Universe. With new resources, their ambitions were to become dominant over all of the other races they shared their Universe with. Their Universe was approaching the point where it reached a point of balance, a resolution of the "what if". This would mean that all of its inhabitants would return to Source. By gaining extra energy, this group hoped to generate a new imbalance and continue their Universe's existence.

What they brought with them were energy frequencies that allowed them to remove freedom of choice, the exact opposite of the energy structures of our Universe.

The Fourteen also brought with them devices designed to collect energy on their behalf. The first devices they used were scattered around the Universe. These were huge structures that were about one kilometre high – see illustration below. These devices were constructed of a shell of energy that contained nothing. A state of 'nothing' cannot exist in this Universe - there is always energy present in one form or another.

Anyone investigating these devices would find that if they approached closely enough, the device would implode inward drawing with it the energy of the soul approaching. It would then use the energy of that soul to create a 'black hole'. Black holes are energy conduits that connect one part of space to another. These devices were programmed to connect one part of space to a predetermined location where the Fourteen could harvest the energy 'swallowed' into the black hole from the area surrounding where the original 'bomb' was situated.

Black holes did not exist in this Universe before these Fourteen bombs created them. They are not a natural phenomenon. In creating the black hole, the bomb's implosion destroyed the soul of the one who approached it. It destroyed the soul and used the energy contained within it to create the black hole. Nothing like this had ever occurred in this Universe before or since.

There was nothing any soul within this Universe could do to resist their wishes. The Fourteen could force virtually anyone to do as they insisted. A huge amount of damage was done to this Universe's resources because of the Fourteen's ambitions. This was the reason why the Universe had shut Earth away from the whole; to try to protect it from the possible damage the Fourteen could cause. Earth had to be protected at almost any cost.

The Fourteen used a number of methods to gather the energies they sought. The implosion devices were the most devastating to souls who tried to oppose their onslaught into this Universe and gathered huge amounts of energy. They also brought with them 'machinery' that were like the kinds of machines used in coalmines to mechanically extract coal from the seam face. These machines mined energy in a similar way and stored it in 'containers' which were then 'ferried' through the original wormhole back to their Universe. These machines seemed to break the energy patterns down to their base frequencies that would then make it possible to restructure the frequencies into something useable in their Universe.

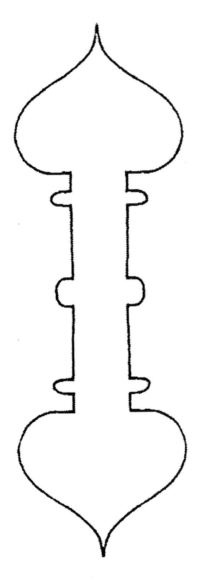

A Fourteen Implosion Device

They could not take the energy structures from us intact, as they would not be useable in their Universe as the two patterns of energy were not compatible.

Almost one quarter of our Universe's energy structures were destroyed in this way. It really was like some kind of mechanical mining process. Nothing like it has been used in this Universe before or since.

They also had energy gathering devices that could work on an individual basis.

On Earth, if one country decides to occupy land that is seen as being part of another's territory, a war usually ensues with the physical deaths of many people occurring as a result. Only humans have developed weapons designed to kill another person. No other race, in any Universe, uses weapons and the Fourteen were no different. If you opposed the Fourteen they did not try to 'kill' you but forced you to work for them in gathering energy on their behalf. This was done by implanting crystal-like devices into the fundamental soul energies of their victim. The original forms of these devices were ones the Fourteen brought with them but as they made their way through our Universe, they encountered the types of technology used by the semi-physical races and made use of those as part of these personal energy gatherers.

These personal devices had several components but were, essentially, a central energy gatherer, a little like a double terminated quartz crystal. This 'crystal' drew to it any energy within its vicinity and stored it in something a little like a battery pack. Attached to this 'battery pack' was something along the lines of a plug-in socket which could be 'plugged into' by one of the Fourteen and the battery pack drained of the gathered energy. The wearer of these devices did not get any benefit from the energy they had collected, they were just part of a mobile machine.

As a further twist to these personal energy gatherers, a smaller version of the implosion 'bomb' device was sometimes connected to them. If any attempt were made to remove the energy gatherers by someone else, the bomb would implode, destroying both souls and creating a new black hole. These devices were not designed as weapons but as energy gathering devices. They effectively became weapons only when attempts were made to remove them.

There was one other complicating factor that proved to be almost impossible to deal with until very recently. The way the Fourteen entered this Universe was by constructing what scientists would call a 'wormhole'. These wormholes are, theoretically, two black holes connected together so that they become open ended 'tubes' of energy connecting one place to another with travel possible in both directions. Black holes only travel in one direction. When this 'wormhole' was constructed from the other Universe, its entry into ours produced a blast of energy, a little like a nuclear explosion. As the blast occurred, 33,000 souls were passing this spot on their way to Earth. All of these 33, 000 souls became caught in the blast and were 'infected' with the energy patterns of the other Universe. In other words, these 33,000 were 'irradiated' with energy frequencies that gave them the capability of removing freedom of choice.

It was always the choice of the individual to make use of these frequencies or not. Many did not, but some did and they brought these frequencies, eventually, to Earth.

Attempts had been made to protect the Earth from the energies of the Fourteen once the full implications of their presence were known. The Orion and the Draco Gateways had been closed and the solar system sealed from outside influences. Unfortunately, those who had been 'caught in the blast' had full knowledge of Earth's existence and were already on their way here. Once they had recovered from the shock of the blast and understood their new potential, they came here breaking through the gateway closures.

The first signs we saw of their presence on earth was about 350 BC. Alexander the Great had empire-building aspirations. Prior to his presence on Earth, nobody else had. Humans, up until Alexander, had been desperately seeking for answers. Whilst there were 'squabbles' between various settlements, there had been no 'wars' or attempts at taking over someone else's territory. Alexander, however, was the first to attempt an act of conquering, an imposition of his will over others. Alexander was the first person to arrive on Earth tainted with the energy frequencies of the Fourteenth Faction and he made full use of them.

Following Alexander, the Romans began to expand out of Italy, as did those out of Mesopotamia, Egypt and, eventually, the concept spread. New leaders emerged who had the ability to take control of the population they led and force them into acts of aggression against others which the population did not want.

The worst to emerge at this time was the Roman Catholic Church. All other Empires have crumbled but the Roman Church has found ways, by intimidation and torture, to maintain its position of control over a large percentage of the human population. The Vatican has systematically and deliberately destroyed as much of human knowledge as it was able to. Many resisted this onslaught and were slaughtered for their efforts. Many libraries of ancient knowledge, such as at Alexandria, were burnt to the ground and the population kept from the true knowledge of human purpose and endeavours.

Many chose not to make immediate use of the energies they had been contaminated with but in more recent centuries we have seen some Royal families and dynasties make use of

Fourteen energy structures and impose their will over the population. As the world has begun to change, we have seen the rise of corporate companies who have taken on global proportions. Pharmaceuticals, chemical and, more recently, biotech companies have taken control over much of what we do and, in particular, control of what governments do, especially in the Western world.

The Industrial Revolution was the epitome of Fourteen aspirations, the stripping of the natural resources of Earth.

Prior to the industrialisation of the Western World everyone lived in harmony, more or less, with the Earth which they worked with to provide food. Once the idea of industrialisation took hold, the world irreparably changed for the worse. No more understanding, no more replenishing, no more working WITH the planet, just the destruction of everything for a reason nobody, to this day, can quite work out: Fourteen energies – the removal of everything this Universe had to offer in terms of resources. Humanity suffered in a way that was never intended and never envisaged. The survival of the Earth was put at risk and the Universe was struggling to find the resources to help defend us.

There are a group of thirteen beings, thirteen souls who act in a 'management' capacity for this Universe. Their role is to balance all energy resources so that the Universe maintains its energetic integrity and so fulfils its intended function. These Thirteen had been struggling. The Fourteenth Faction were a development which could not be planned for. Neither was there an immediate answer in how they could be dealt with.

The blast from the initial wormhole had sent energetic ripples across the Universe, the only good thing about this 'blast' was that it allowed the Thirteen to read the Fourteen's energy 'signature'. Once this signature was known, the Thirteen set about finding ways of building new energy structures that were the equal but opposite of the frequencies the Fourteen had brought with them. If the Fourteen's signature could be matched with sufficient force, they could be expelled from this Universe.

The task the Thirteen undertook was like trying to conjure something out of nothing. The energy frequencies that made up the Fourteen's 'signature' do not exist in this Universe. Somehow, the Thirteen had to find a way of building matching frequencies from the energies that DID exist in this Universe, a seemingly impossible task. But, they did achieve it. However, finding a way of matching these frequencies brought with it its own dangers.

The Thirteen are not free-ranging souls. They are a fundamental part of the functioning of the Universe and, whilst it could be considered that they exist everywhere, they are really such a part of this Universe that they can be viewed as forming the Universal envelope. An ability to be everywhere at the same time whilst also rooted to the spot, so to speak. If the Thirteen unleashed these new energy frequencies it would alter the fundamental make-up of this Universe and freedom of choice would disappear, causing this Universe to catastrophically collapse in on itself.

They had created thirteen free-ranging souls specifically to be 'Guardians' of the thirteen original planets within this solar system but they could not be contacted because of the closure of the Orion Gate. However, four of these Guardians had returned to the Thirteen when the planets they were Guardians of decided to leave the solar system and these four were put to use.

Although free-ranging, these four were aspects of the Thirteen and acted with the integrity and energies of the Thirteen intact; it was felt that they would not be corrupted by being imbued with the copy of the Fourteen energies. Ultimately, this turned out to be incorrect but at last this Universe had a means of fighting back against the Fourteen.

These four turned out to be immensely successful in their new role. By presenting the Fourteen with their own energy patterns, they could be overcome and the Universe was rapidly cleared by sending these people back to the Creationary source. However, some of the Fourteen had found ways of disguising their energy signatures by cloaking themselves in frequencies that related to this Universe. These proved to be more difficult to track down.

The problem with trying to hide something is that, sometimes, it can make it more obvious and this is what happened with Earth.

Earth's Guardian is known by many names. In South America he is known as Zamna, in North America as Wohanna Wish Hey, in Eastern lands as Enoch, in Greece as Mercury and in the West as Merlin. All the same person.

Earth's Guardian's story is told in *Planet Earth – The Universe's Experiment* but it is sufficient to say that 'he' did not know anything of this struggle with the Fourteen as he arrived on Earth shortly before the Fourteen wormhole was formed.

Everything in this Universe is ultimately determined by what happens on Earth. Whilst the Thirteen were trying to resolve the problems at a Universal level, the four guardians tracked the Fourteen wherever they went within this Universe and, eventually, all tracks led to Earth.

This is where the problems of one guardian becoming corrupted with Fourteen energies eventually became apparent. Huge problems occurred within human history because of this particular errant Guardian. Earth's Guardian was misled, misdirected and effectively sent on a wild goose chase for many hundreds of years because one who was part of the Thirteen used Fourteen energies to send 'him' off the track.

This is not the reason behind the concept of 'Satan' being a 'fallen Angel'. Such concepts belong to human made religions and not to Universal events or characters.

In the end, it was Earth's Guardian who recognised the energies for what they were and took steps to counter the threat to Earth.

The final act of this 'war' for Universal survival took place on Earth in March 2002. Very few, on Earth, are directly aware of these events.

The Fourteenth Faction have been destroyed and all of their energy patterns removed from Earth and from the Universe as a whole and returned to the Creationery source.

The final acts of this struggle have been completed and no more can this Universe be threatened by outside forces.

As for everyone on Earth? We are now back on track as the forces which pushed us into unwanted directions are now gone. Despite these delays and distractions, we can still regain the Human Template in our allotted time frame. There is no need to panic!

Chapter Six

Other Forms of Interference

The Earth exists in order to explore the possibility of 'physical' life. The forms of life on Earth, in all of its diversity and splendour, outnumber all of the other forms of life throughout the whole Universe. Life has found abundance in its physical expression far beyond any expectations or even dreams. Nobody could imagine what forms and numbers of species Earth would eventually develop when it began its exploration of 'physical' life twenty five million years ago.

The scientific viewpoint is that life began on Earth somewhere in the region of 3,000, 000,000 (three thousand million) years ago. At the beginning of scientific investigation into the age of life on Earth, several scientists independently arrived at a calculation of 25 million years. This figure was modified over the years, as the scientific community could not fit all of their theories into this short a time-span. When Carbon 14 dating was invented, the time-frames did begin to fit their theories and so was adopted without too much in the way of verification.

Carbon 14 is a radioactive version of carbon. It was noticed that the radioactive pieces, contained within the rock containing the carbon, decayed to particles of lead. By calculating the average proportion of radioactive particles against lead particles, they believed they could calculate the rate of decay, the 'half life', of this material. By knowing the 'half life' they could work out the age at which something died.

The main flaw in their calculations is that since the 1930's we have dumped an unbelievable amount of lead into our atmosphere. Lead pipes, lead toothpaste tubes and especially the lead in petrol has saturated every aspect of human life and contaminated everything. If a rock or bone sample is washed in a laboratory before being prepared for testing, it becomes contaminated by the lead particles in the water giving a very false decay reading making the sample appear much older than it actually is. The problem is made worse in other ways. If a palaeontologist finds a dinosaur bone at a 'dig', unless the excavation is carried out under totally sterile conditions, and the bone then continues to be treated and examined under sterile conditions, it will become contaminated not only by the lead in the water and atmosphere but also by the DNA of those who handle it. The DNA will be passed on from the sweat on someone's palm, from their breath if they blow on it and numerous other potential contamination processes.

This means that virtually every Carbon 14 or DNA test carried out by scientists is flawed, giving dates and results that are fundamentally misleading.

As with all of the planetary consciousnesses of our Solar System, the Earth took up its position thirty-five million years ago. It took ten million years to construct the 'shell' and prepare it for life.

Whilst developments were taking place in our solar system, other developments were occurring elsewhere throughout the Universe.

Our Universe came into being a little over fourteen thousand million years ago. At its point of Creation, all of the energies and souls needed to give the Universe shape and form were created with it; these were the Galaxies, Stars and Planetary levels of consciousness.

About one hundred million years ago, the individual souls of the six non-physical races were created to bring independent free-moving life to the Universe. However, whilst they might be free-ranging and capable of travelling anywhere within the Universal void, they could only have limited interaction with other souls. This is meant in the sense that whilst they could communicate on all levels, they could not 'physically' interact with anything. This presented limitations that could not be overcome in their natural soul energy state.

The next stage of development was to bring into being those who could take care of the more 'physical' aspects of the day to day running of a Universe and so the seven semi-physical races were created thirty million years ago.

These are Earth related time-frames, not Universal time-frames. What this means is that ninety-eight, or so, per cent of the souls who are currently in human form were first created one hundred million years ago, there is no such thing as 'an old soul': everyone was created at the same time. Those who originate from the semi-physical races are thirty million years old. Older is not better, just different. This does mean what it says. The vast majority of souls who are in human form were first created one hundred million years ago. All were created at the same time. The remainder of humanity, those souls who are of semi-physical origin, are thirty million years old.

The first of the semi physical races to develop forms of travel beyond their own energy 'bubbles' were those who originated on NGC 584. These had developed skills as 'genetic engineers' on their own worlds and they began to put their knowledge and expertise to use on behalf of the Universe.

The idea of genetic engineering either engenders fascination or horror in human minds. This is mainly to do with our individual and collective memories of the time towards the end of Atlantis. Fascination by those who undertook the experiments, and horror by those who were experimented on or saw the effects of the experiments. Either way, it was not a good time in human history.

The Human Genome Project and the work carried out by Biotech companies are an echo of the Atlantean experiments. The people who head the biotech companies are trying to repeat the mistakes they made on Atlantis but without the ability to seemingly understand the implications of their actions. They are also acting from the viewpoint of greed and profit which makes many of their decision-making processes flawed. They do not act for any kind of 'greater good' for humanity or the planet; just mistakes made for profit. The threat of GM organisms and their potential for wiping out all life on Earth is the only thing that can stop humanity completing its task. If these GMO's end up with free reign across the Earth, then the resulting genetic meltdown would mean no viable life anywhere on Earth.

The NGC, however, do not work for profit.

When the Earth felt ready to begin developing its ideas for the life that it wanted on the planet, it was the NGC who responded. By twenty five million years ago, the NGC had amassed a considerable amount of knowledge about developing forms of life. They also stored the genetic 'blueprint' for every life form that existed throughout the Universe.

To bring life forms from another world is comparatively straightforward as the form already exists - all that is required is that it is modified to suit life on the new world. But with our Earth, it was a question of starting from scratch and that is a great deal more difficult.

The first problem was how to generate a suitable atmosphere, an atmosphere in which physical life forms could breath. The obvious answer was to use bacteria. Bacteria are beings that can take one form of a gas and convert it to another. Many, many forms of bacteria exist throughout the Universe because of their 'exchange' capabilities and so the NGC chose the most suitable and made the required modifications to suit 'physical' life. The next question was how to introduce them?

There is always debris floating around in space. Odd bits of old planet, the occasional lump of rubbish or comets. Comets have a consciousness, they know who and what they are. Essentially, they are beings who are prepared to travel, acting as carriers for various substances that might be required on other worlds. Think of it this way: a consciousness builds around itself a shell of ice; ice, within space terms, exists at a temperature of absolute zero. This is the perfect temperature for carrying 'living' material. In terms of Earth's requirements, this was the perfect transport mechanism.

It works like this: seed a comet with a living organism, allow the organism to cool to a temperature where it is dormant, all of its life processes close to zero. When the comet impacts with a planet's surface, heat is generated and the organism returns to life.

This is what happened with Earth. By carefully choosing impact sites across the whole of the planet's surface, the new atmosphere-generating bacteria could be evenly distributed. On impact, the comet explodes, releasing the bacteria into both the air and the ground around the impact site. By using a number of comets, the whole of the Earth's surface was covered almost instantaneously; allowing the chosen bacteria to be seeded everywhere.

The comet's consciousness, having done its job, leaves the surface to form a new ice ball and the cycle begins again. Unfortunately, this large number of comet impacts has led to a number of 'dents' in the Earth's surface leading scientists into many wrong conclusions. With the process of building a suitable atmosphere begun, it was then a question of letting the bacteria do their job.

Water was formed from chemical reactions and atmospheric condensation. The original design for the atmosphere was completed after about fifteen thousand years. The next stage was finding forms of life that could take 'physical' density.

The whole Universe was searched and a progression of life forms tried. Some very successful, most failures. This is Earth's history of life's development, trial and error. Acceptance and rejection, creation and evolution and on going development. Just development and rejection of the unworkable or the ones that did not show the required promise.

Only one 'mass extinction' has occurred in Earth's history. That was three and a half million years ago when four planets decided to leave the solar system. The impact of the planets' decision to leave resulted in the loss of virtually all life on every planet, including Earth. It is at this time that the dinosaurs disappeared. All other life developments or removals have occurred by the Earth's choice.

Earth's purpose was to build a human - all other life was incidental to that goal. This is not to say that all other life on Earth can be sacrificed to the main aim. The exact opposite is true. As Earth has developed, souls who have taken on human form have made their choices; all of the other life on

Earth is part of the planet. This life is so diverse, so exceptional, so abundant and so precious that it is humans who are now the ones that can be sacrificed to save the rest. Make no mistake about this. Human life has been proven to be possible on Atlantis and so the Earth has fulfilled her primary function already. She is just waiting for humanity to catch up with reality and the original Atlantean human template. If we fail in our aim to regain our full human form, the Earth and its created life will still survive but humanity, as we currently know it, will not – see later.

The first visitors to Earth were of the six non-physical races who came to observe progress, followed by the NGC who came to help develop and create new life. As others of the semi-physical races developed the ability to travel between galaxies, they came to help the NGC and the Earth in all of its early developments. The Sirians came next, closely followed by the Pleiadeans, all to help this experiment of Earth take shape and form.

All of the other planets in our solar system were also helped in this way. The period from twenty-five million to fifteen million years ago was extremely hectic in terms of life development and creation. Everything then settled down and all of this solar system's forms of life, an immense diversity, were allowed to evolve.

All of the thirteen planets harboured and nurtured life. Some forms were adopted by all of the planets, whereas most were original creations of each of the planets' consciousness. The solar system was alive and thriving.

The following years of the history of the solar system and Earth's are chronicled in *Planet Earth – The Universe's Experiment* and so we can now bring ourselves up to date on more recent 'visitors' to our Earth.

Every – well, almost every - soul that has taken on human form originates somewhere other than Earth. The vast majority of human souls have come here from the six non-physical races with a smaller percentage made up from the NGC, Pleiadeans and Sirians. Many others have visited but remained in their original soul state.

However, we have also been 'visited' by others of the semi-physical races and it is these visitors who have brought about the UFO phenomenon.

The first of these were a race we have come to call 'The Greys'. The Greys originate on a star system many galaxies distant from us. Like the NGC, their own name for themselves does not translate into anything pronounceable by the human voice box.

These beings have been observing Earth for many centuries and an extremely small number have tried taking on human form. Currently, there are about one hundred and fifty "Grey" souls in human form. They have become fascinated by the forms of life on Earth and in particular the human body form. They see their bodies as weak and in danger of not surviving for very much longer. The Greys are the ones who are taken as the archetypal "alien": short, slender bodies with a grey leathery skin, not too many facial features and large black eyes. These beings do not have large black eyes. Their eyes are pale yellow with vertical irises, a little like the eyes of a domestic cat. On their home world they live in subterranean complexes and so their eyes are very light-sensitive and wear the equivalent of 'sun glasses' when subjected to any kind of light source, hence the large black eyes.

The Greys live mainly on energy sources rather than on any kind of 'solid' food. They also have a rudimentary emotional response to situations. They are not aggressive but can respond to situations on an emotional level roughly equivalent to, let us say, a chimp. This is not a derogatory comment, either to chimps or the Greys, just trying to find a comparison. The Greys behave a little like human teenagers in that they have a certain level of knowledge but cannot quite put it into context.

In coming to Earth, they found two things. First the human body form and, secondly, the human emotional debris. Humans have become so emotional that there is a separate layer within the mass consciousness that is comprised of a cumulative layer of human emotions. To the Greys, this is a banquet of 'food', an emotional energy source from which they have freely fed. This is not something nasty, it is just that we humans are so emotional that it creates layers of energies within the mass consciousness that are superfluous to human needs; all the Greys do is make use of this excess energy.

The first real contact we had with these beings was with the Roswell crash in New Mexico in 1948. This was an event where a Grey ship malfunctioned and crashed into the desert near the town of Roswell. As with just about anything that happens in America, the military took control. The crash provided them with an alien ship and three survivors. The Greys were reluctant to become involved in human affairs but the American military had three of their beings. So began a relationship that continues to this day. The American military looking for 'advanced' technology to give them global military advantage and, in return, the Greys received free access to the genetic material available on Earth. Abductions and animal experimentation began at this point – on the say so of the American military. This is why so many of the reports of UFO sightings and animal mutilation as well as human abductions occur in the States – with military agreement.

The Russians also have their 'Roswell' crash, it is not Tungusca (see below), the crash occurred in the Ural Mountains far away from the assumed site. The Russians rejected the Grey approaches which were based upon their agreement with the Americans. The Russians did make use of some of the Grey technology but they would not give agreement to human or animal experimentation.

In genetic experimentation terms, the Greys eventually realised their limitations and they looked for outside help. In this search they found another group whose name is not translatable and so we call them 'Blues'.

The Blues are unusual in their form. Amongst the semi-physical races, the Blues are unique in that they have body hair. Five out of the seven semi-physical races have no hair at all. The Pleiadeans have blond hair, but only on their heads, the whole of their bodies are otherwise free of hair. The Blues, on the other hand, are covered in short dark blue hair all over their bodies. They are only about three feet (1m) tall and have a barrel-shaped body with very short legs. This might begin to sound like the description of a pantomime character but they are extremely intelligent with a specific interest in genetics.

The Blues and the Greys began working and travelling together some time ago and it is the Blues who are trying to help the Greys achieve their goal of a more human body form. It is the Blues and Greys together who are responsible for the huge number of human abductions and animal mutilations that have taken place over the past sixty years.

To assist them in inter-galactic travel, the Blues developed a symbiotic life form. These life forms 'live' inside their ships, like a living lining to the hull. When they embark on the huge journeys necessary to come to Earth, the Blues step inside pockets within this living hull which then sustains and protects them through the duration of their journey. Control adjustments of the ship are made psychically whilst the Blues are in a form of stasis within the cocoon of the living hull.

Whilst they have not been particularly aggressive towards humans, they have caused confusion and disruption to the Human Plan. Both of these races have been banned from entering our solar system for the past couple of years which has resulted in a massive drop in UFO sightings and abduction claims.

Other groups who have visited have come to try to help steer us through our reintegration process by providing hints and clues as to the directions we should be taking.

The Pleiadeans, for example, have contacted many people on Earth over a number of years to try to pass on knowledge about what we are up to. A great deal of the information provided by the Pleiadeans has been misinterpreted by those who they contacted and this has led to misunderstanding and confusion. Many assumed, or hoped for, a 'landing' by the Pleiadeans on Earth and these hopes were widely circulated in the 1980's and 1990's. A landing in their natural state was never the intention of the Pleiadeans. We, humans, are attempting to sort ourselves out and find our way back to being what we were on Atlantis, the original human template. We are close to completion of this process. The Pleiadeans know that if they landed in full sight, they would distract and detract us from our plans and we would not complete our intended learning process.

Many, on Earth, know that we are close to our intended goal but are insecure in the role they have chosen to play. Would it not be so much simpler if the Pleiadeans landed, if Jesus returned or if there was a new 'Meritreia'? That way people could offload their responsibilities on to someone else and they would not have to complete their work. The Pleiadeans are not going to land, unless there is some very dire and immediate threat to the Earth and those who claim to be the new Meritreia are misguided or have an ego problem.

The soul who was Jesus, the King of the Jews, did return. In that new lifetime, he tried to take on the same role, that of freedom fighter for his peoples. His name that time around? He was given a name that meant 'son of Joseph' at birth but later changed it to Yasser Arafat. Nothing is what it seems, only choices made by the souls involved.

We are on our own. We will make our own mistakes or failures but there are those who are quietly trying to help.

Since the mid 1950's a 'peasant' farmer in Switzerland called Eduard Albert Meier has been in contact with a group of Pleiadeans who call themselves Plejaren. These are a branch of Pleiadeans in the same way as a Chinese or Australian could call themselves a branch of humanity. Nobody, not even so-called 'professional' debunkers have been able to prove that the information or photographs in the possession of 'Billy' Meier are anything other than genuine. Over the years, the Plejaran have provided extremely accurate predictions of world events up to twenty years before the events occurred.

Another Pleiadean 'branch' that has contacted a number of people on Earth call themselves Ummites. These beings are from a planet they call Ummo. They are extremely polite and have encouraged those who they have contacted, usually by letter, to be extremely sceptical about their presence. They have also provided extremely accurate information that is connected with scientific observations and the theories being explored by Quantum Physicists.

The Pleiadeans have a role throughout the Universe along the lines of a 'diplomatic corps'. They are involved in virtually everything that occurs on a Universal level. They are helping us on Earth to arrive at our chosen conclusions, but at a distance. They do not interfere. Nor do they tend to contact people very often but they have had three massive ships in permanent orbit around the Earth since the mid 1970's to provide help where and when required and are on 'standby' in case it looks like we will totally destroy ourselves. The Earth will not allow self-inflicted total destruction on humanity and so the Pleiadeans will only step in at the request of the Earth's consciousness.

In more recent times, the Earth and humanity have seen themselves coming under a new threat. The first physical knowledge we have of these beings was in 1988 but their observations of Earth stretches back about 200 years.

In 1988, Tass, the official Russian news agency, published a series of articles which were picked up by various 'quality' newspapers in several countries. This was a very unusual news event which was only reported on once by the *London Times*.

The item was this: a number of craft of non-terrestrial origin had landed in several Russian parks. From these craft came beings who were about eight foot tall and who wore blue 'tin foil' environment suits. They just stood around in the parks but if anyone approached them they raised 'stick-like' objects held in their hands and 'aimed' them at those who were approaching and they suffered some kind of paralysis which froze them to the spot and they woke up several hours later with a severe headache.

The landings in America or anywhere else were not reported in the press. These beings are a semi-physical race who call themselves Velon and originate from a planet they call Velus.

Many human mediums have reported having communications from beings who claim to originate from 'Venus'. These are the same peoples - they have deliberately chosen not to correct this misunderstanding. Whilst Venus did support beings equivalent to humans, they have not existed for three and a half million years and so these communications could not possibly have come from a Venus origin.

The Velons developed craft capable of inter-galactic travel about one thousand years ago. As they began to explore the galaxies around them, they encountered the primary energy flow between the Thirteen Beings (Universal 'management') and our solar system. The Velons misinterpreted this as being an energy flow direct from the Creationary source to somewhere that must be 'God's chosen' place or peoples.

This misunderstanding brought about the formation of something very similar to a kind of 'religion'. Nobody, throughout the whole of the Universe, has developed a belief process similar to what we call religion. All are aware of their Created beginnings and their place within the Universal Soul but none have found it necessary to 'worship' on any level. This made the Velons unique throughout all of the Universal civilisations; humans can be considered an exception to any rule.

The Velon belief structures led to the formation of six religious 'factions' each believing their version of events to be the only true version and each wrote their own form of 'bible'. These differences of opinion and doctrine led to many disagreements and a form of 'war' although their war did not involve the killing of any of their peoples, more a kind of 'shunning'.

Each of the six factions developed their own ships and tried to find the ultimate end of the energy flow to claim it for their own. If the Velons were not living on God's chosen planet, they wanted to claim the one that was for their own and each faction wanted to be the first to 'claim' Earth for their followers.

The first of the Velon ships finally arrived at the Orion Gate about two hundred years ago. The energy stream they had followed clearly led them directly to Earth but the behaviour of its inhabitants did not fit in with any of their versions of

'God's Chosen People'. As far as the Velons were concerned, something very strange was occurring here and they decided to begin by observing rather than attempting to land. In any case, the Earth would not have allowed them to come any closer, neither would any of her 'Guardians'.

The method the Velons chose for close observation of human life has led to the greatest internal problem this Universe has ever encountered.

The Velons use a variety of technological tools in their everyday lives. To human eyes, these 'tools' look more like an energy form as they are obviously designed for use by a race which is semi-physical in structure. These 'tools' can be implanted into a human body and the person carrying them will have no awareness that they are there. The Velon approach to implant these devices into humans was to request that a soul on their way to taking on human form carry a 'tool' for the Velons without giving the full explanation of what the 'tool' was for. This was the beginnings of an extreme form of subterfuge.

At the beginning, the Velons asked a soul on its way to Earth if it wanted to have a device that would help it with the life it was about to embark upon. Most souls took this at face value and accepted the device as a gift. Once it was realised that the Velon offer was not quite what it seemed, the Velons began to find ways of implanting their 'tools' into humans without their knowledge or their consent.

These tools were communication devices, a little like video cameras. If one had been implanted, it would automatically transmit sounds and pictures of everything the wearer saw and did back to Velus. This 'filming' and transmission would occur in real time. As you were living your life, everything you did was transmitted back to Velus as it happened and as you experienced it.

This Universe is built around the 'what if' of absolute freedom of choice. Every soul that exists within this Universe has the absolute right to choose its course of action. What a soul of this Universe cannot do is to act in such a way that it removes the ability of another soul to choose its own actions. Yet this is what the Velons were doing. By not informing souls of the true purpose of the communicators, they were removing free choice. By implanting these communicators into people without their consent or knowledge, they were removing free choice. The souls which were implanted in this way were those which had formed soul to soul 'Links' on Atlantis. These energy Links are located between the physical self and the higher self and, given the physical distance between the two souls, this link could be broken into and the devices implanted.

The Fourteenth Faction came from another Universe, bringing with them the energies from which they were naturally constructed. They could do nothing other than remove freedom of choice as it was a fundamental part of their make-up. The Velons had no such excuse. Their religious fervour had pushed them to the point where they were prepared to break the only 'law' that exists within this Universe and they knew that they were doing it.

The Fourteenth Faction caused a considerable amount of damage to this Universe (see later), but the Velons shook this Universe to its foundations to a point where the Universe was at the point of collapse and would return to Source. If those on Earth were not so close to completing their goal, there would have been no hesitation - the Universe would be no more.

Each soul within this Universe is connected, on one level or another, and under particular circumstances all can communicate to each other. This ability was put into use to try to find a solution to how the Velons should be dealt with. This is the ultimate form of democracy. Each soul has a vote and every single soul within this Universe was asked for its opinion. We on Earth also voted but most are not consciously aware of the vote taking place as this was done by our 'higher selves'.

Ninety eight per cent of the Universe voted for the expulsion of the Velons, this included the Velons themselves. The other two per cent wanted to give the Velons a chance to redeem themselves. This was actually attempted but Velon actions since the vote, or at least actions taken by the Velon 'religious' leaders, have shown that there cannot be any reconciliation. This is what is currently occurring. The Velons are being expelled from this Universe. This Universe will lose a whole race by the middle of 2005.

This step has never been made before and, hopefully, never again. It was only taken because the Universe's choice is to see humanity complete its chosen task. The amount of restructuring taking place within our Universe is beyond our comprehension (see later) but we are being given every opportunity to bring The Human Plan to its hoped for conclusion.

There is one other source of problematic interference as far as completing our plans is concerned and that is purely man-made.

Since the early 1950's, American foreign policy has become increasingly dominated by a group who have become known as 'Neo Conservatives'. This group has a core membership of about ninety people with many hundreds under their influence. This group's intentions lie in their extremely right-wing Christian beliefs. This group believes absolutely in the Bible. Their main focus of attention is in the final book of the New Testament, Revelation, particularly the section on Armageddon. This section of Revelation was written about the year 560 BC when the Jewish nation was under the control of

Nebuchadnezzar. This apocryphal piece was written to encourage the Jewish people to fight off their enslavers by promising salvation by God leading to the destruction of all non-believers once the Jewish lands were returned to their control.

This Neo Conservative group have interpreted this part of the Bible to mean that once the lands 'covenanted' to them by God were back under Jewish control, it will trigger the events leading to Armageddon occurring. These lands cover Israel, Palestine, and parts of Syria, Iraq, Kuwait and Egypt.

When these lands are once again under Jewish control, God will ascend the 'true believers' to heaven whilst the non-believers tear themselves apart on Earth. Once the non-believers' destruction is complete, the 'ascended ones' will return to Earth and become God's chosen people living in a 'golden age' for one thousand years.

The foreign policy decisions taken by several American presidents in the last fifty years have all attempted to bring about the scenario that triggers Armageddon, the current president, George W Bush, being particularly enthusiastic to fulfil this group's wishes.

Occupation of the 'covenant lands' will not lead to much of anything, not even for 'true believers'. But the attempts to regain control of these lands is causing death and misery to many thousands of people worldwide. It is also distracting us from our true purpose and intentions, that of completing the human plan.

As a footnote to this chapter, the events that did occur in Tungusca in 1908 need to be clarified. Many 'UFOlogists' like to claim that this was Russia's equivalent of the American Roswell UFO crash. In fact, the truth is even stranger than they claim.

Tungusca is a region of Siberia in Russia. On the clear, sunny morning of 30th June 1908, a meteorite entered the eastern sky and exploded before it hit the ground. The many thousands of eyewitnesses reported 'huge lights' and sounds like 'cannon fire' over a period of nearly an hour. Some eyewitnesses, very close to the event, reported seeing huge, bright balls of fire and the 'sky opening' so that they could see the stars beyond.

What these people witnessed was a defence system that has been rarely used since it was installed twenty thousand years ago.

Meteorites exist in vast numbers in a band beyond the orbit of Saturn. Every once in a while, these lumps of rock collide with each other and send one of them shooting out into space. On very rare occasions, one of these displaced rocks will approach Earth.

Many thousands of very small meteorites fall to Earth each year causing very little damage as they are usually burnt up in the atmosphere. However, some of these meteorites can be several miles across and it is meteorites of this size that this defence system was installed to protect the Earth from.

The system is semi-automatic in that any large meteorite approaching Earth orbit will be detected and if it is large enough, the system will respond and fall under the direct control of the Earth's consciousness.

Essentially, the system comprises a network of generators over the whole of the planet's surface. The ones located in the target area are 'switched on' and they generate large balls of 'plasma' energy that are powerful enough to destroy the threat. The Earth generates and controls as many of these 'energy balls' as are required to destroy the meteorite.

The first ball to strike is the most powerful and it is designed to use sufficient force to break the meteorite into smaller pieces. The resulting 'explosion' is then vented off into space, hence the account of a 'tear' in the sky. The larger fragments are then destroyed by the other balls released.

The system works very efficiently but enough energy was released onto the surrounding area to totally flatten trees for two thousand square kilometres.

Chapter Seven

New Life, New Directions

The human population at the end of 2004 stood at 5,896,000,000 (five billion, eight hundred and ninety six million). Of these souls in human form 108,000 were of Pleiadean origin, 98,000 of NGC origin and 17,600 of Sirian origin. There were other races represented in the form of 156 of Grey origin and 220 of Velon origin. The remainder, the vast majority, were souls from the six non-physical races, the so-called 'Angels'.

Except, not quite. There are other souls living on Earth in human form we have so far not mentioned. There are currently fifteen of these souls in human form out of a total number of souls, in the whole of existence, of one thousand two hundred and fifty six.

These 1,256 souls are very, very special.

In the way that a soul can originate, first come into creation, on, say the Pleiades they would be described as Pleiadean in origin. These 1,256 souls are First Born; their place of Creation is Earth.

The First Born began their story on Atlantis.

The human template was developed as the 'standard' pattern that any soul wanting to live as a human being on Earth needed to 'adopt' in order to achieve their wish. With the human template fully developed and completed, the next stage of human evolution could begin.

The Thirteen Beings who maintain balance within this Universe have the capacity to Create primary forms of life on behalf of the Creationary source. In order to bring about these new souls, the Thirteen worked through their representative, the 'Guardian' of the Earth, the one known as Merlin. It was he who took on the task of drawing the energies through from the Thirteen and began the process of creating new souls whose home is Earth. Initially, only eight were created to see what the new souls were capable of and how they reacted to the very unusual physical nature of the Earth. These first eight were immensely successful and the other 1,248 followed very quickly.

It is difficult to describe the differences between the First Born and the other souls who have chosen to take on the human template. They are fundamentally the same but with one major exception, the First Born resonate precisely with the energy frequencies of the Earth. No other soul, of any origin, quite fits the energy structures of the Earth in the same way; these are perfectly matched and perfectly attuned to everything of the Earth.

The original plan was to create many thousands of these souls so that the Earth had an 'indigenous' population but, by this time on Atlantis, we had begun to realise that we were having problems and so the plans were put on hold until such time as there was full awareness of where the problems were coming from. When we destroyed Atlantis, the First Born naturally stayed on Earth to undertake the massive amount of repair work needed.

It is not always easy to look at Universal developments with anything other than human eyes. There is a Universal Soul, a soul that is this Universe. Every living thing that exists within this Universe is connected to, and is a part of, the Universal whole.

From a human perspective, we would see there being a 'hierarchy' within the beings that inhabit this Universe. This really is not the case. Except for the Fourteenth Faction and the actions of the Velon, everything that has occurred within this Universe has been part of a planned development, the chosen path of the Universal Soul. The Development of the First Born is a natural progression of this chosen path. Nobody is seen as being 'above' another and certainly nobody is seen as being 'beneath'. Every soul that inhabits this Universe is seen as equal and the same is true for the First Born. They have taken their place within the Universal whole and have been welcomed with open arms by all other souls.

The First Born are not here to usurp the current human population. The Earth needed 'hosts' to welcome in visitors from other worlds and show them the ways of being human. All are welcome to visit Earth, as long as they fit into the human template. We, who are currently in human form, undertook a task on behalf of both the Earth and the Universe to try to reconstruct the original template and we have nearly completed our job.

When we returned to Earth, 20,000 years ago, the First Born were here to welcome us back. Like all souls, the First Born are free to travel where they will throughout the whole of the Universe and choose to take on any form available, but they decided to stay with the Earth.

As the souls who had returned to Earth began to experience the difficulties described previously, the First Born were there to help. As a soul perfectly attuned to the frequencies of the Earth, they did not suffer the same 'slowing' as everyone else did.

By about eight thousand years ago, we were as we are now and we took our steps to find our answers by designing a new human template and undertaking our Karmic lifetimes. The First Born could not fit into the new template. They were so in tune with the Earth's energies that they could maintain the original template quite readily and the new template caused them too much disruption on a soul level.

This unexpected development meant that the First Born could play little part in our knowledge gathering experiences. If the First Born took on a human life using the original template, they would shine out like beacons of energy and cause major disruption to our plans to find the answers to our problems. The way in which human nature was already developing meant that anyone who appeared to have knowledge or wisdom was held up to be a great 'Soul' and a great leader. If the First Born took on such roles, it would lead to a dependency on the First Born for leadership and answers that would totally disrupt the Karmic process.

They have helped whenever and wherever they have been able to but we were already having enough trouble with religious leaders that it was considered too unsafe to allow the First Born to be amongst the new humans. They, sadly, had to just watch and wait until we had completed the task we had undertaken on the Earth's behalf.

Over the past few years, those who are on Earth and are taking an active role in the Earth's development, have come to realise that they are 'here to do a job'. This is true. The job is to find a way to the conclusion of our chosen task. To find the answer to the question we asked ourselves seven thousand years ago. We are here to find a way for any soul who chooses to come to Earth to fulfil their full potential when they are here.

The human template we have been used to for the past seven thousand years does not allow us to be who we really are, nor can we fully appreciate the wonder that Earth truly is as we have to leave three-quarters of our souls outside of the body. It is only when we have achieved our aim of fitting the whole of the soul into the physical body that we will fully realise that we have been working on behalf of the Earth, helping her achieve her aim of her own 'children'.

There have been several times when we could have completed our knowledge - gathering process during the past seven thousand years and this has given some of the First Born the opportunity to re-take human form. This they have done with great joy but, as we failed each time, they have tended to return in very small numbers at the start of each potential time of change.

As noted above, there are currently fifteen living on the planet, mainly concentrated in Britain. Most are experiencing great difficulties in fitting into the modified human template even though it is rapidly being changed back to the original template energies. Several of those who were born a little too early have committed suicide as they could not cope with the template frequencies nor could they find understanding amongst their fellow man. Of the fifteen who have returned, thirteen are currently under twelve.

As we bring the Human Plan to its conclusion, a great many changes are taking place on Earth. The Earth herself is bringing about situations where she is able to act in ways of her choosing.

The first action that has been recently brought into play is that her 'children', the First Born, are set to return. Not only to return, but for new souls to be created as 'Earthlings'. Most of the original First Born will be reborn into western cultures over the next few years as we regain the original template.

But new souls have already been 'created' for Earth - new 'First Born' are arriving. These will be born to traditional tribal cultures in various isolated locations around the Earth. The first thirteen mothers to bring in these brand new souls are already pregnant with this very special new life and were set to give birth in August 2005.

As humanity moves forwards, more and more First Born souls will be created as we fulfil the promise made to the Earth on Atlantis.

All of our hard work of the last seven thousand years has allowed us to find our way back to fitting into the original human template. As more and more people reintegrate their whole soul, the more the Earth can act. The more we regain our original aims, the more the Earth is set free. As we progressively fit the whole soul back into the physical, the more we give back to the Earth and the more she can act in the ways in which she wants.

The new First Born are not the only new life to come into being on our Earth. Other forms of life are also arriving. Some were previously extinct, some are entirely new.

In Universal terms, the Earth is a very new planet. As far as the Earth herself sees it, she is still experimenting with the forms of life she wants to inhabit her surface and so animal or plant extinctions occur as the Earth readjusts her view.

With the destruction of Atlantis, all of the life in the Northern Hemisphere had to be modified to suit conditions of winter. Many species were removed, at the Earth's request, at that time. Those who remained were, to a certain extent, experimental. Some species have proven to be too weak to continue and have followed a natural line to extinction whilst some have been made extinct by the unthinking actions of humans.

There are huge changes and readjustments being made throughout the Universe (see later) and the Earth is also undergoing adjustments of a similar magnitude. Not all of the life that is currently on the planet will still be here in five thousand years by the choice of the Earth. There will also be new species developing which have never been seen before. Whilst we humans have failed to take our responsibilities for animal life seriously, we are not entirely at fault for the current level of plant and animal 'readjustments'.

The Earth has taken a view that is wider than we can currently see. Whilst this does not absolve us of our responsibility, it does start to put what is currently occurring into a different perspective. There is no doubt that humans have been responsible for the destruction of thousands of plant and animal species. Destruction of habitat for greed has taken a huge toll. But, if the earth wishes to have these species back, the NGC can reconstruct them - it will just take a little time.

The Earth is also beginning to make new choices: her dialogue with the NGC is ongoing. There is continuous assessment of each life form and new niches are always there to be filled.

The Earth has recently taken a new form of life, never before seen on the planet. The most common form of delivering new life are comets. It is not currently practicable to allow a comet to hit the Earth as it would cause too much disruption at a time when we humans need as much peace as possible to complete our plans.

A few years ago a new comet entered our solar system which the astronomers called Schumaker Levy. It carried with it the new life intended for the Earth and its 'payload' was delivered as close as possible to us without actually impacting on the Earth. Jupiter allowed the comet to strike its surface but fragments travelled to Earth. These fragments were carrying a new form of life. They hit the ocean just off Mindanao in the

Philippines. This is one of the deepest sections of the oceans of Earth, the Mindanao Trench. The species 'delivered' in this way is a form of crab that is suited to life under the extreme pressures these kinds of depths under the sea produce. These are not ordinary crabs. They are consciously aware. They know who they are, where they are and what they are. Their evolution should prove to be interesting.

Other species that have been extinct for up to three hundred years are now back on the planet. Even the dear old Dodo is now alive and well on an Indian Ocean island and survived the Tsunami.

Nothing is forever, just readjustments or new developments.

Whilst we are on the subject of choices, even the question of Global Warming is not a man-made problem. Since the industrial revolution we have spewed millions of tons of toxic chemicals into the atmosphere. Even so, the Earth has dealt with this. The current atmospheric changes are not down to human pollution but to planet choices.

If you look at the make-up of the gasses that are forming the Greenhouse Effect you will see that ninety-eight per cent are caused by 'natural causes'. In other words, from volcanoes and gas emissions from the ground. This is definitely not to support George W Bush's concept on the subject of industrial emissions, just the reality of the situation.

The atmospheric changes are occurring because we need an atmosphere that is different to the one we have been breathing. We also need to remove the ice from the North Pole. There will be some consequences to these changes for all life, particularly within the Northern Hemisphere. These changes are occurring in an effort to regain the balance we once had on Atlantis.

The skewed global axis is shifting back to vertical and the atmosphere is shifting along with it, all planned by the Earth and all planned as part of the concluding chapters of the Human Plan.

There is, however, the problem of man-made pollution on the planet's surface that is our responsibility. The millions of tons of industrial waste, nuclear waste and oil spillages need to be cleared up by us. This is not something we can do successfully before we complete our reintegration process. When we have completed our plans, we will all be equipped to deal with this abomination by psychic means. Any attempts made before we complete our changes will not be effective.

If we were capable of clearing up this mess before we completed, all we would do is allow the polluters to continue. With the atmosphere and surface in its current mess it is, at least, forcing people to look at the issue and begin to realise their responsibilities.

Chapter Eight

Changes Beyond Our Earth

Some of the changes that are, and will be, occurring on Earth were looked at in the last chapter. There are other modifications also arising to Earth, the Solar System and the Universe beyond. In response to our arriving at our answers, the Universe is acting to bring back balance to all.

To begin with Earth.

As humanity is finally beginning to shake itself out of the past and into a new consciousness, the Earth is travelling with us. At the end of its initial formation, the Earth was about one quarter of its current diameter. As she began to make way for the life forms she had planned, the Earth began to grow in size. This was the planet's own consciousness expanding to welcome in the new life. As life developed, the Earth continued to expand until by the time she was ready to welcome in the new souls who were to take part in the experiment of humanity on Atlantis, she was about ten per cent larger in diameter than now.

As we humans expand in our levels of consciousness, the Earth is expanding with us. Literally, the planet is getting bigger. This rate of expansion is currently at about 50mm (2ins) per year. This might not sound like very much but the rate of expansion is accelerating as we approach a point where we can fully integrate the higher aspects of our consciousness. By the end of 2011 the Earth's diameter will be as it was on Atlantis.

There have been many such expansions and contractions during the planet's history. These cycles have been caused by changes in life choices made by the Earth herself as she readjusted the life she wanted to support. By shrinking in size, a proportionately larger sea area than land area could be experimented with bringing around large shifts in relative sea levels. These sea area to land area changes also altered atmospheric and temperature mixes allowing experiment-ation in the gas mixtures of the atmosphere and the forms of life that the atmosphere supported.

When the Earth was hit by the debris of two planets, roughly three and a half million years ago, she was forced to shrink to about half the current diameter in order to conserve her energies in an attempt to recover. This amount of shrinkage also raised sea levels sufficiently to literally 'wash clean' the surface in order to start again.

As the planet begins this new, current, phase of expansion, it sets up major stresses within the crust as the regions around old fault lines bring about new land. This expansion leads to earthquakes and volcanoes.

There are a number of groups of people, mainly in the western world, who consider earthquakes to be too dangerous to human life and, by working psychically, have attempted to prevent these types of events from occurring. In doing so, they have generated points of abnormally high stress within the Earth's crust which means that when earthquakes do occur, they are of a far higher magnitude than the original earth-quake had it been allowed to occur naturally. This problem has become so great for the planet that it was necessary to vent off most of this stress during September 2004 as the Earth knew that if the pressure was not relieved, the resulting earthquakes would have been catastrophic on a global level. Had these stresses not been vented, huge volcanic eruptions would have occurred in several countries triggering dust clouds large enough to bring about a 'nuclear winter' situation. Given humanity is precariously poised ready to make our final steps to full consciousness, the Earth was not prepared for this level of disruption to occur when we are all so close to our collective goal.

It does seem to be a human trait that we will tinker with things we do not fully understand and cause far greater problems than if we had left well alone.

The upper levels of our atmosphere are changing in ways that are not related to CFC emissions, other pollutants or the planet's own emissions. There is a new layer of what the scientists call HO gas forming. This is a totally new layer within the atmosphere. Although this gas was there before, it has never been present in such quantities.

Away from the Earth, other major changes are occurring.

The moon now has an atmosphere. The scientific name for the gas that makes up this totally new atmosphere is 'Natrium'. It is currently six thousand kilometres deep and appears to be growing.

Each of the planets within our solar system has a consciousness in the same way as Earth. As we begin the final phases of the Human Plan, the energies that have sustained Earth are slowly being diverted to the other planets. As this energy is received, the other planets are undergoing an awakening of consciousness. They are all changing in one way or another.

As each planet's consciousness begins to re-awaken after their three and a half million year sleep, they are beginning to glow measurably more brightly in the night sky. All of the planets are also undergoing shifts in their polarity and their magnetic flow is increasing.

Their atmospheres are altering either to give a new mix of gases, where an atmosphere already existed or, as in the case of Mars, the atmosphere is twice as dense as it was a few years ago. This is why several of the recent missions to Mars have failed as the ships have tried to enter an atmosphere denser than they were designed to fly through.

Recent photographs taken of Jupiter show a 'tube' of luminous energy, ionising radiation, between itself and its moon Io. This tube of energy has never been seen before.

The Sun is also undergoing a shift in consciousness to match that of the planets. Its magnetic field, called the heliosphere, stretches around all of the planets in the solar system in a 'tear drop' shape. The energy emissions making up the leading, blunt, end of the teardrop have been measured to have increased by a factor of one thousand since 1963.

There is also a new planet within the solar system. This is one of the four planetary consciousnesses that caused all of the damage three and a half million years ago when they decided to leave the solar system. This is the planet that was located between Venus and Earth. NASA has been plotting the course of this planet for some time and has christened it Planet X. Its real name is Sedna.

The planet is currently in its consciousness form. That is, it does not have any physical density, just its soul energy. It is not yet decided whether it will take on physical density and become a 'whole' planet again – another potential change. It has moved back into its old position to try to help the Earth regain its original vertical axis by adding its gravitational pull to help the Earth pull itself upright. The Earth's axis has already returned to vertical, in an energy sense: it now needs to follow the energy with the physical. This should be achieved by about 2009.

Everything within our solar system is preparing itself for change. Change on Earth and change within the Universe, as a whole, is reawakening dormant life.

The changes occurring throughout the Universe are on a scale far too vast to fully imagine. To explain some of what is going on, we start to fall into the problems of Universal time structures and how they relate to time as measured on Earth. Several major events have occurred very recently in our time-frame but the reality can range across many millions of years in Universal time depending on which part of the Universe the events took place. The only way of explaining these events is to put them into the sequence in which the events occurred. Each event triggered a sequence of subsequent events but they did not all happen in order of time as we would measure it. An event could have taken place five years ago in our time-frame but ten thousand years ago in another part of the Universe. Whereas an event that took place six months ago, our time, took place one million years ago in Universal time.

The Fourteenth Faction

All of the beings who invaded us from another Universe have been evicted from ours together with all of their 'machinery'. All of their primary energy structures have either been destroyed or ejected from our Universe.

As these primary energies were removed, many events began to take place. 'Black Holes' are collapsing. These were 'holes' in the fabric of space created by the implosion devices the Fourteen brought along with them. As these devices imploded, not only did they destroy the souls who triggered them but they also rent huge rifts in the energy of the fabric of space around them. As the Fourteen energy patterns finally dissipate, the Black Holes are collapsing and the regions of space that were damaged are being repaired.

Those who carry Fourteen 'energy gathering implants' are finding that their impact is lessening as they begin to dissolve (see later). All of these devices will have finally dissolved by 2009.

The damage done by the Fourteen's energy gathering 'machines' is immense. Approximately one quarter of this Universe's energy reserves and potential has been destroyed. This loss of energy potential brought us to the very brink of total collapse. This means that if the damage had been any worse, this Universe would not have been in a situation to sustain itself and it would have collapsed in on itself leading to the destruction of all Universal life as we returned to the Creationary source. The problem was that serious.

The last of the Fourteen were destroyed by allowing them to believe that there existed an immensely powerful energy source available on Earth that they had not detected. As soon as they entered our solar system, their energy structures were condensed to a point where they could not act and so they could be 'captured' and held.

When the Fourteen broke into this Universe, they did so by creating a 'worm hole', a back-to-back black hole. As they burst through this wormhole, thirty thousand souls on their way to Earth were contaminated with the energy structures of the Fourteen. This allowed these souls to make use of these energy patterns and remove freedom of choice. As they were on their way here, they brought those energy patterns with them, causing major disruption to the Human Plan.

There was always choice as to whether these thirty thousand made use of these frequencies or not. Most chose not to. Of those who did, their loss of ability to make use of these frequencies is reflected in the rise in success of those who campaign against Globalisation and the activities of Trans National companies.

The Thirteen Beings who maintain the balance of energies of this Universe are currently at work restructuring the whole of the Universal 'envelope' so that our place in Creation is maintained for as long as possible. If our solar system, with its 'dense' energy patterns, did not exist, the Universe would have failed. Another question we humans answered.

The Six Non-Physical Races

With the realisation that humanity is capable of a great many things, together with the Creation of new First Born souls, there are many who originate in the realms of the Six non-physical races who consider their role in this Universe to be complete.

The Six have experienced difficulties in finding a true role within this Universe. In their natural pure energy state, they are capable of travel to anywhere and within any time in this Universe. They can experience what it is to be something but not what it is to touch something. If one came to Earth, in their natural state, they could 'feel' what it was like to exist as, say, a flower. They could 'step' inside the flower and feel all of its energy flows but they could not smell the flower's scent nor could they pick the flower.

Whilst the Six have been involved in everything that has occurred within this Universe, they have been unable to take a fully active role. Whilst the concept of existing in a state of pure soul energy can be appealing, it does mean that they have become detached from the day to day 'workings' of the universe as the only role they can take is that of an observer. They cannot use 'tools' of any kind and so cannot take a full role in reconstructive work.

The choice to return to the Creationary Source is one that is being freely made on an individual basis. Nobody, anywhere, has forced this issue. This is entirely free will in action. Those who wish to remain active within this Universe are doing so; they will not be leaving until they choose it is their time. To put it into another context, some of the 'Angels' are returning to 'God'.

Those who have chosen to take on a human 'suit of clothes' will continue to have their choices. They are free to remain on Earth, as long as they fit into the Human Template, or they are free to choose to explore any of the other experiences this Universe has to offer. Always free choice.

The Velon Peoples of the Planet Velus

The fate of the Velons is very different to that of the Six.

The Velons deliberately and consciously chose to act in ways that removed the freedom of choice of others. Their actions broke the only 'law' that this Universe functions under: nobody can act in a way that removes freedom of choice. In terms of this Universe, this 'crime' is so heinous that it cannot be overlooked or forgiven.

Once the activities of the Velons were known, every race made their attempt to get them to change their ways. The Velons made many promises, but their determination to 'take over' the Earth has not diminished. Every attempt to find a way to help them failed. Even when the consensus vote was for their eviction, many still tried to reach a compromise. The Velons refused to co-operate.

By the middle of 2005, virtually all of the Velons had been removed from this Universe. The Velons who remain will be those who have been granted 'political' asylum on Earth and their future fate is still to be fully determined.

This is an act of extreme sadness. The whole Universe mourns the loss of these peoples but the action had to be taken otherwise this Universe would have had to return to Source. The Velon activities alone would have brought this Universe to a state where its existence would have been in doubt. To break the fundamental energy patterns in this way could have led to total collapse. Coming on top of the destruction wreaked by the Fourteen, there were insufficient resources to overcome this level of imbalance.

With the loss of the Velons, Earthlings, the First Born, will now take their place as the thirteenth race of this Universe.

Chapter Nine

The Process of Change

There has been a great deal of discussion over what is meant by 'change'. Many speak of a process of 'Ascension', others of moving into the 'Fifth Dimension'. The term 'Ascension' implies we are moving out of our bodies, somehow, into a place somewhere 'beyond'. Whilst the talk of the 'Fifth Dimension' is to fundamentally misunderstand the make-up of the soul and the energy frequencies of which the soul is comprised.

We, humanity, are not 'Ascending' to anywhere and the 'Fifth Dimension' would relate to the third chakra, just about the level of the navel. What we are doing is bringing the Higher Self, the rest of the soul, back into the physical body. If anything, the exact opposite of 'Ascension'.

When we (humans) first arrived on Atlantis, we developed an energy matrix into which the soul needed to fit in order to call itself a human being, the 'Etheric Template'. This template determined organ positions and the energy frequencies needed to become 'physical' on this Earth. This is what it means to be a human being, what the soul needs to do to take on human form. Eight thousand years ago we made a modification to the etheric template to the one we are currently used to. This modification was meant to be a temporary condition and made us, in the eyes of the planet, sub-human.

What we are now attempting to do is to move ourselves out of this sub-human state and back into the original Human Template first developed on Atlantis. Not ascension - just reintegration.

The original Human Template was very different to the one we have become used to using. The whole of the consciousness, the soul, was contained within the body. This means that there were no specific energy points, or Chakras, along the spine, just a smooth flow of soul energy. We had our full complement of memories intact giving us thirteen strands to the DNA spiral. Our bodies were slightly less dense than they are now and we could communicate psychically with all living things.

We could survive on extremely little in the way of 'solid' food, a couple of pieces of fruit and something like seaweed could sustain us for the whole day. We could transmit our thoughts to any other human anywhere on the planet and, if we wished, we could take the body along the thought to relocate ourselves anywhere on the Earth's surface of our choosing. We were 'super human' in comparison to what we have become. This is what it means to be truly human.

The revised template we adopted seven thousand years ago is very different.

The soul is currently divided into two, the 'physical self' and the 'higher self'. This division in our consciousness was necessary in order to overcome the loss of the higher aspects of consciousness we had been experiencing.

We had thirteen energy points or chakras. Seven within the physical body and six that connected us to our higher selves. The purpose of the seven physical chakras was to allow the higher self to communicate with the physical. Each chakra relates to a specific group of organs and to an aspect of our lives. This new template and its chakra functions was first designed and mapped for us by the humans who lived in the region of ancient Sumeria about thirteen thousand years ago. Every single human being who has experienced physical life for the past seven thousand years has adopted this template. Regardless of skin colour or ethnic origin, every single human being is identical. What makes us individuals is our consciousness.

The division between the higher self and the physical self is that about seventy-five per cent of the total soul is not in the physical. In other words, we are used to living our lifetimes with only one quarter of the total soul within the physical body.

The seven physical chakras, their locations and functions were discussed in chapter four. What we need to look at here is the way in which the chakras are changing and why.

Traditionally, the chakras had specific colours which each person adopted. The first was coloured red, the second orange, the third yellow, the fourth green, the fifth blue, the sixth indigo and the seventh violet or white and occasionally gold. These colours reflect the frequencies at which the chakras functioned, red being the lowest frequency with violet the highest. As we progress through our various stages of change, the frequencies of the chakras are changing and, consequently, their colours. Colour is purely a function of frequency. As we raise our energy frequencies, the colours have to change to keep pace.

Not one single person alive on Earth today has these traditional colours. The last person to have these colours died at the end of 2002. There are several stages to our re-integration process and each stage brings with it new soul energy frequencies and new colours to the chakras.

For most people, this process of change began on the 14th of August 1996. Some began a little before then, some a little later. This was the date on which the new primary energy source was connected to the planet. This energy source was designed to 'fire up' this process of change and to remind us all that we had a job to complete.

The first thing this new energy did was to speed up the communication between the higher and physical selves. This was achieved by bringing the six higher chakras into the body and connecting them to the six lower physical chakras. This process had two effects. Firstly, it altered the fundamental frequencies under which the chakras function and, secondly, for want of a better way of describing it, the higher self was now situated on top of the head.

Bringing these higher chakras into the body altered the chakras to an intermediary colour stage. Instead of the whole chakra being a single solid colour, they all now took on a range of colours.

The first chakra has a background colour of a coppery gold. As the chakra spins, 'ribbons' of other colours appear within the spiral. These ribbons have three colours: clear gold, violet and blue.

The second has a background colour of 'petrol' blue; the kind of vivid blue that appears when water is poured on to petrol. The spiralling ribbons here are violet, clear gold and the copper gold of the first chakra.

The third has a background colour of 'petrol' green and its ribbons are coloured violet, gold and blue.

The fourth chakra is where the colours change a little more. The background of the vortex becomes totally transparent. It is a little like the heat haze 'shimmer' that can be seen on hot summer days rising off very hot surfaces. As this transparent shimmer spins, a large number of 'flecks' appear of all of the other colours: violet, clear gold, copper gold, petrol blue and petrol green.

The fifth chakra also changes to the same transparent background as the fourth but the number of coloured 'flecks' reduces a little.

The sixth chakra is also transparent with a very few 'flecks' of the other colours.

The seventh chakra changes to a total transparency. No colours, just pure soul energy.

Most people currently have these intermediary colours.

This first stage of change was an almost automatic process. Very little effort was required to achieve this level of change. Those who chose to remain at the old colours had to actively resist against these new energies.

What these new energies did trigger in people was a desire to resolve old issues. Where issues had been left dormant or ignored in the past, they now began to surface. These issues could be the need to look for a new job, to finally resolve an old family squabble, to divorce a spouse or it could present old issues on a country level.

Most resisted these pressures for resolution - after all, they had been an issue for a long time, perhaps even centuries, so why should I be the one to sort out everyone else? But the sense of pressure grew. Those who totally resisted came down with the final message a soul can give, a terminal illness. Those who did work with their issues to clear them, found their lives changed beyond measure and these were the ones who moved on to the next stage of change.

The more that was cleared, the more the higher self could reintegrate with the body and this produced another change to the chakra colours.

Each and every one of us has the ability to clear our lives of all of its accumulated debris. Those who were bold enough to look at their lives and make the necessary changes and clearances found that all of their chakras became transparent. No colours at all, just pure soul energy flowing through their bodies. This is the stage that everyone on the planet should have been at by the end of 2003. We are human, and to be human is to err.

This process of clearance comes down to one thing in the end: how honest are we with ourselves and with those with whom we share our lives? Total honesty results in total change; partial honesty results in partial change. We can no longer 'play' at our lives, this lifetime is where all of our rehearsals, all of our past lives, have to be put into the final production. We have no time left for further practice.

Those who found sufficient courage to step from their past selves and into an honest present found that their chakras changed again. This time, they disappeared.

These honest people brought so much of their higher selves into the physical that there was instantaneous communication. Once this point is reached, the chakras become superfluous and the communication from your soul is immediate. Magnificent and scary, all at the same time.
But, this is not the final stage.

The final stage is when the remainder of the soul enters the physical and the original Human Template becomes triggered. There are people who have already achieved this. On June the 2nd 2003, the first sixty-eight people made this final step. True human beings once again walk this Earth.

Two groups made these first steps to completion. One in Europe and one in North America. The European group was made up of 43 people of all ages. The group in America was made up of 25 people, again of all ages. Whilst the European group remains safe the American group was arrested on the day it completed and has been experimented on ever since. This group's fate is not so good.

Branches of the American military and secret services have been experimenting with psychic capabilities for many years. Much of the 'Cold War' during the fifties, sixties, seventies and eighties was won, by both sides, using 'remote viewing' techniques. Many of these kinds of techniques are used to carry out psychic attacks on groups and individuals around the world. These are not very pleasant people.

The American group was taken into custody and moved to a part of Edwards Airforce Base where experiments have been carried out on members of this group, three of whom have been killed by the experiments.

Knowledge of this capture and experimentation has spread throughout those who are in a position to make the final steps to completion. Psychic communication really does work, and it has made many understandably reluctant to make the final step.

What must be remembered is that the group in America had been fully aware of the psychic monitoring by the military. They knew that they would be arrested and experimented on. They allowed these events to occur in the hope that it would prevent any other group or individual from being taken into custody in this way. They have been 100% successful in their efforts; no other individual or group, who has undergone completion, has been taken into custody. Those souls who were physically killed by the force of the experimentation will shortly return to human form.

However, not all is doom and gloom. The Akashic records that at the end of 2004 there were nearly 1.5 billion people ready to make these final steps spread out over the whole planet's surface. A total of 250,000 people, globally, have also fully completed their transitions.

What these figures show is that whilst there are those who wish to maintain the status quo and prevent these completions from occurring, the process is now unstoppable. As each individual takes their final steps to completion, the more the balance tips in the direction of human reintegration and the more the Earth responds to our changing consciousness.

Chapter Ten

Transitional Problems

It is clear, on one level or another, to every single person on the planet that we are in a state of change. Many know something is going on but are not too sure what. Some want change but are not sure about how to bring change about. Whilst others are fully embracing their new-found aspects of consciousness and are fully working with the new energies.

Whatever each individual's level of understanding, this change of consciousness is bringing with it some symptoms that have varying levels of emotional discomfort or even physical pain. Everyone on the planet is feeling something of these symptoms of change, some more than others. Not everyone is feeling the same things. For some, the process of change is comparatively straightforward whilst others are finding themselves in extreme pain.

All transitions are difficult to deal with. A transition is a change from one state of being to another and anything that brings about change can be uncomfortable. Change of the magnitude we are experiencing will inevitably have consequences.

To start with the simple ones

As we take in more and more of the energies of the higher aspects of the soul, the rate at which the soul communicates through the body increases. As the higher energies become part of the physical tissues, the organs begin to lighten in density. Our grandparents' generation could totally ignore the soul's promptings through the chakras and body organs and they could store their emotional debris away in the appropriate organs either until they died or the organ became so dysfunctional that it was surgically removed.

We do not have that kind of luxury. As the organs lighten in density, there is no available space to hide the emotions any more and so we find ourselves becoming very much less tolerant of situations we ignored in the past, in addition to which symptoms of illness are arising very quickly.

The medical profession cannot deal with the numbers of people now seeking medical help. Whilst there are secondary factors such as chemicals in foods or pharmaceutical drug residues, the real reason is that the soul wants us all to be totally honest and deal with each situation as it arises. It is this pressure from the soul that is making people ill as they try to resist the need to change. If you go with the wishes of the soul, no symptoms arise. If you try to ignore the soul and try to carry on as before, the more the body begins to fail.

Even if we do try to work with our higher aspects, some of the bodily changes also bring about symptoms, some of which can be uncomfortable.

One common one is extreme tiredness. There appears to be no real reason for suddenly becoming much more tired than usual, especially as you are living your life as normal. The reason for the extreme tiredness is that the cells of the body are also undergoing a change of density and this requires the body's systems to work much harder than normal, resulting in physical tiredness.

Vegetarians and vegans are finding that even after many years of a diet that is vegetable based they are beginning to crave meat. The reasons for this are the same as the tiredness. As the cells change their structure the body's energy requirements rise and the best way of meeting the body's needs is to eat protein. This sounds a little paradoxical. If the body's structures are becoming lighter, why does it need heavy protein? This is because the cells require physical energy - the type of energy derived from food - to power-up this change. The best way to feed this extra energy need is with heavy proteins in the form of meat.

Other changes are a little less dramatic. The hair and finger-nails begin to grow at an alarming rate. This is because the body is rejuvenating every single cell in the body and those cells that are used to growing constantly are accelerating in their rate of growth.

Levels of intuition are improving. Most people are beginning to find that they instinctively know the truth about a situation no matter how the situation presents itself. A lie will now be seen for what it is rather than accepted as in the past.

The reason for this change is that the brain's psychic centres are waking up. However, with some people this growth in intuitive awareness can cause problems. These psychic centres are located both sides of the brain and there are four in total. One just above and behind the ear and one at the base of the skull, just above the junction with the neck. Two centres each side of the head. These psychic centres are enlarging in size, which means the brain is getting slightly bigger. As the brain size increases, the skull also has to enlarge slightly. People who wear hats, for example, are finding that their favourite hat has become too tight and they need to buy a new one, one size larger.

However, if the bony plates of the skull are fused together, as they are with most people over the age of thirty, this increase in brain size can cause huge pressures within the head resulting in severe headaches. These headaches are usually centred in one of two places and sometimes both. These are just above the bridge of the nose and at the top of the neck. The pressures in these locations can be enormous and the headaches excruciating. The pressure can affect any part of the head and neck. They can even result in jaw ache and toothache in teeth that your dentist will tell you are perfectly healthy, as well as move from tooth to tooth.

Not everyone is getting these headaches so if you are not do not worry, it does not mean that you are not changing, just that your skull has proved to be a little more flexible. If you are having these headaches, the best way of dealing with them is to have a scalp massage with the massage as deep as possible. The other way of dealing with them is to consult a cranial osteopath who has techniques to gently ease the plates apart.

Another symptom is one of heart flutters and shortness of breath. These are not serious problems but can be worrying if you experience them. These symptoms are brought about by changes to the heart chakra as it adjusts itself to the new energy structures. The heart chakra is also the energy centre used by the soul to communicate to the physical body. As the speed of communication continues to increase, the chakra needs to constantly adjust its function. If you experience these flutters, they usually last for about ten days and then disappear but they can reappear a couple of weeks later. There can be three cycles like this possibly spread over a period of up to six months.

The symptoms listed above are very common although not everyone is experiencing them, whilst some have them all. They are all temporary and will not last for very long. They can be quite frightening when you experience them, especially as the medics have no answers as to why they should occur. Try to bear with them and accept them as symptoms of improvement and change rather than symptoms of problems.

Use your common sense over these symptoms. If they persist for any length of time, you should consult a doctor/healer/ homeopath/herbalist etc.

If you are not experiencing these kinds of symptoms, do not panic. It just means that your higher self has learned from the experiences of others and has found ways of getting you through the changes without distress.

The above problems are not the only situations that are occurring in people's systems. The ones listed above are very common and can apply to virtually everyone.

The ones below are very different.

They are listed here because they are problems some are encountering but it must be stressed that they apply to less then one per cent of the population. If you have any of these problems, you will recognise something of them within yourself. If you do not have these problems then you will probably think that they are too far fetched to be genuine. They are very real and can be devastating in their consequences.

As we progress through these changes of energy, a searchlight is being shone on to every single cell within the body as we reintegrate and renew. If there are no issues or problems, the cells just rebuild and the searchlight moves on. However, some people carry a legacy from their past and this legacy can have consequences.

This legacy can manifest itself as genuine, but unusual, physical symptoms or there might not be any symptoms, just a sense of 'block' and despite all efforts to clear these blocks, you cannot seem to move past them.

Virtually everyone who falls into this category is a soul whose origins lie in the semi-physical races. This means that no more than two hundred and fifty thousand people, globally, will have these kinds of problems.

Atlantean Chips

The first of these kinds of devices is also the one that has the capability of causing the greatest physical problems. These are genetic programme chips that were first used on Atlantis to accelerate Cro Magnon man into the original human template.

These chips were used to experiment with the human form on Atlantis to see how the body could be adapted or altered to suit whatever designs the person who programmed them wanted. The chips have been reproduced each lifetime since Atlantis as they became a fundamental part of the individual's genetic (DNA) memory. However, they have usually remained dormant as there was insufficient soul energy within the body to reactivate them. There have been notable exceptions in the past such as the alterations made to the face and body of the 'Elephant Man'.

Most of these chips have remained totally dormant since Atlantis until this lifetime. As we moved into the twentieth century, we had the perfect opportunity to undergo our reintegration process. By the 1920's, there was sufficient energy and impetus to trigger the changes we recently began. As these energies began to take hold these chips began to be reactivated and people began to be born with unusual genetic modifications.

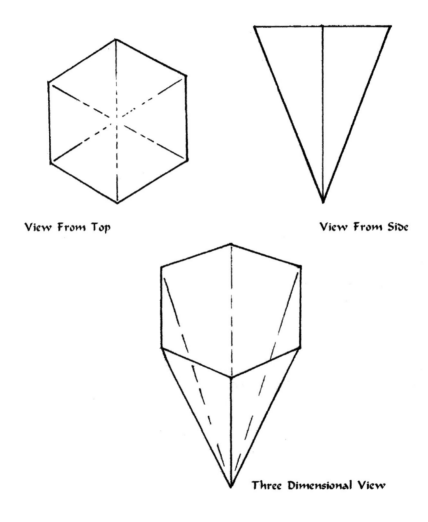

View From Top

View From Side

Three Dimensional View

An Atlantean Chip

The chips can be triggered at three different times in peoples' lives. Firstly, within the womb, which frequently leads to the fetus being spontaneously aborted by the mother or the child is stillborn in an attempt by the soul to deal with the problems these chips can generate by allowing the modifications to occur. Once fetal development has completed, still-birth will occur in the hope that allowing the chip to fulfil its programme sequences will remove the DNA memory allowing the soul to be born again very quickly clean and clear of the problem – this does not always work.

Secondly, the chip's programme can be triggered at puberty. Puberty is the time when the last piece of the soul to be brought into a particular lifetime enters the body and this additional surge of soul energy can trigger the chip's programming and physical body alterations begin at that point.

Thirdly, the chip can be activated if there is a particular trauma in someone's life. A trauma only occurs because the soul wants it to. If the trauma is successfully weathered, the additional energy gain can trigger the chip.

Many people have lived sixty to seventy lifetimes since Atlantis and each new body the soul has constructed has included a copy of the original chip. Like a computer programme, each time the chip is copied, it allows scope for a corrupting of the programming and so most of these chips are not as powerful as they were when first designed and implanted. This means that only some of the original modifications occur.

The types of potential modifications are limitless. Some are subtle hormonal changes whilst some can be major structural changes to the whole body. There is nothing predictable about these chips as they were designed by the individual who carries them.

Regardless of the physical modifications, another problem with these particular chips is that they are shaped very much like a prism and, like a prism, as the higher energies of the soul try to enter the body, they encounter the chip and the energies become scattered, causing problems - usually down the arms but also an inability to 'ground' the energies properly. This lack of grounding can lead to a sense of dislocation from life, an unconnectedness that can be very uncomfortable.

Another problem is that as we progress through our changes, the higher self begins to download its accumulated memories of all of our lifetimes. This memory download is the reason why our DNA is changing and growing in size. Very few people on the planet now have only two strands to the DNA spiral, most have at least five. As this download progresses, those with these chips can find they will have full memories of events which they know did not happen in this lifetime but the memories feel as if they have, leading to a great deal of confusion over what these memories actually represent.

All in all, these chips are capable of massive disruption to someone's life and body. The only way of dealing with these chips is to have them removed by a healer who is familiar with these kinds of devices and the DNA needs to be reprogrammed to 'forget' having the chip.

Sirian Chips

Sirian chips are totally different from the Atlantean chips both in design and intended function. They are also much younger in their time of construction and adoption by individuals.

When we set the Human Plan into action seven thousand years ago, we were embarking on a series of lifetimes where we would, hopefully, learn how to be human. At that stage in

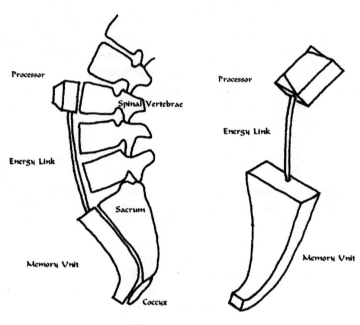

Processor

Spinal Vertebrae

Energy Link

Sacrum

Memory Unit

Coccyx

Processor

Energy Link

Memory Unit

Chip As Fitted On Spine   **Three Dimensional View**

A Sirian Chip

our history we were very much as we are now, i.e. we had two
spirals to our DNA memories. Given that we needed as much
memory as possible in order to record our experiences and
accumulating knowledge, our semi-physical friends from
Sirius suggested that they design a tool which would make up
for our lost eleven thirteenths of memory.

These chips seemed like a good idea at the time but we had forgotten that the higher self recorded everything for us anyway and, as it turns out, these chips were superfluous.

These recorders are located at the very base of the spine and have two components. The first is a 'lozenge' shaped device that acts a little like a microphone. This component picks up everything that occurs within the individual's life by monitoring all of the activity that takes place within the spinal column. Energy movements, nerve impulses, hormone activity, all are monitored. Once the 'microphone' has picked them up, these impulses are recorded in the other part of the device that acts as a 'tape recorder'. At the end of each lifetime, everything that has been recorded is downloaded by the higher self and added to our store of memories.

The problem with these devices is that once an event has been recorded, the device thinks it is a part of your make-up and no matter what is done to resolve a problem in life, if it becomes cleared, the device realises that it is now missing and will reconstruct the problem.

For example, if you had a particularly stressful childhood, your adrenaline levels would have been very high whilst the body prepares itself for a 'fight or flight' situation. As your life progresses, your adrenaline levels will remain permanently high regardless of how settled and non-threatening your life has become.

Another example of the kinds of problems these chips generate is to do with life situations. You may find yourself with a problem where you have done everything possible to resolve it but you then begin to start remembering aspects of what had occurred. As the thoughts about the problem return, you begin to think that it could not have been fully resolved as it has now come back to mind. As you begin to consider the problem again, you have to look at it from a wider and wider perspective. In this way, instead of the problem going away, it becomes bigger and bigger and keeps returning no matter what actions you take to clear it. This is the chip at work. Once it has recorded something, it thinks it is a part of you and will keep putting it back.

Galaxy Chips

This device is the main tool used by the NGC in their genetic work. They have been christened 'Galaxy Chips' as they look a little like a spiral galaxy when viewed from the front.

These devices are immensely complex in their construction and function and were first designed about three hundred thousand years ago.

There can be quite a number of problems arising if you happen to carry one of these devices. When used by the NGC they are immensely useful tools but they are not designed to function in the kind of dense-bodied beings we humans have become. These devices are built on to the spine between the shoulder blades and they connect directly into the central nervous system through the spinal cord. Every nerve in the body connects into the central processor and is acted upon by the programme sequences contained in the outer ring and then the nerve impulses travel back into the spinal cord and into the hypothalamus and brain as normal.

Physical problems include movement of the spine between the shoulder blades that can result in nerve pressure in the arms and it can also give symptoms similar to a hiatus hernia.

If you undergo a strong emotional trauma, the nerve impulses travelling up the spine can be too strong for the device to handle and it will send the impulses back to the originating organ creating an emotional loop. If you find yourself in a situation where you are physically threatened, particularly if

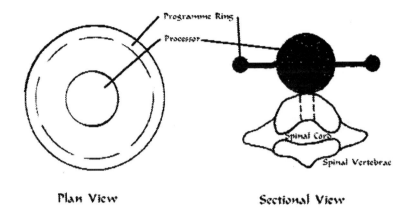

An NGC 'Galaxy Chip'

this occurs in childhood, you can trigger the device to build a protective energy field that totally surrounds the body. This field can then trap the emotion of the situation within it and the emotions can never be cleared. If this protective aspect is triggered, it literally puts a protective wall around you which makes it very difficult to have a close, loving relationship as a potential partner will feel rebuffed each time they try to become closer to you.

The chip is also a communication device powerful enough to allow psychic communication across the width of a galaxy. Human psychic communication centres are not yet redeveloped enough to make use of this function but the tool still tries to do its job. If you are in a position where your 'heart goes out' to someone, this device will attempt to communicate with them. This produces an energy bridge between you and that person, or animal, and if that person ever thinks of you again, they can draw energy from you along this bridge. What this means in practical terms is that you can end up totally exhausted and feeling drained for no apparent reason.

Every single soul who originated on NGC 584, and is now in human form, carries one of these devices but they are also carried by others. All of the souls who remained on Earth immediately following the destruction of Atlantis, to help undo the damage, will also carry one of these. The tools were essential for the kind of genetic alteration work that was needed to be carried out to help life in the northern hemisphere to survive.

Multi Dimensional Chips

These are, again, of Sirian design and construction. They are designed to generate energy fields that can encompass one thousand dimensions. They have a very practical and useful function when used as they were intended to be used but can generate extreme problems in humans.

The semi-physical races can travel virtually anywhere they please within this Universe, however, if they came to Earth in their natural state, we would probably not see them at all as our brains are not tuned to 'read' the frequencies at which they exist. We might, if we had an enhanced psychic potential, see an energy outline but we would not see much in the way of facial detail.

The same applies if the semi-physical races travel to the realms of the non-physical races: they would appear to the 'Angels' as physically dense as we appear to the semi-physicals. This chip can adjust these problems.

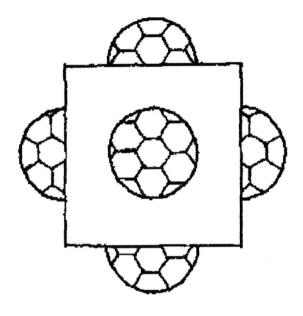

A Sirian Multi Dimensional Chip

What they do is to adjust the energy structures of the semi-physical wearer so that they appear in their natural semi-physical state wherever they travel. So, for example, if a Pleiadean wanted to come to Earth and appear as they do naturally, they would trigger this chip and they would appear as solid to us as they do to each other. The same applies if travelling to the energy structures of the non-physical races; these chips can adjust their energy frequencies in the opposite direction so that they still appear in their natural state.

These are devices of immense complexity but when worn by someone who has adopted human form, they can cause problems. These devices are situated in the throat, just below the line of the jaw. It can make the wearer feel like there is a constant obstruction, a 'frog', which needs to be cleared. However, if sufficient energy has been put through the chip it can cause the energy to react as if hitting a prism, resulting in too much energy in the head and a lack of energy below the throat chakra. At its extreme, it can cause a vortex to form making the wearer feel like they are in a constant spin with the head and higher energies disappearing into the neck region, an extremely unpleasant feeling.

All of the chips described above were freely chosen by those who carry them. Most of the people who do have these energy tools were the ones who have remained on or near Earth since the destruction of Atlantis. They were devices deliberately chosen to aid them in their chosen reconstruction works. Generally, these souls have remained with the Earth ever since - if they had returned to their home worlds, they would have left their 'tool kit' behind before returning to re-take human form. It is very sad that the ones who have done the most work to help the Earth and humanity are the ones who are now suffering as we undergo our transition.

Before we began our climb back to our true consciousness, these tools would have been dormant, as there was insufficient energy within the physical body to activate them. When we have fully completed our transitions, these tools will again be useful and can be fully made use of. It is this transitionary stage where the problems arise and why these tools need to be removed from people's systems.

The following two sets of devices were not chosen by the ones who have them implanted; these were imposed against their will or they were tricked into taking them into their bodies.

The Fourteenth Faction Energy Communicators

When the Fourteenth Faction exploded into this Universe, many of the souls here tried to prevent the Fourteen in their energy-gathering processes. Instead of causing these souls any kind of harm, the Fourteen forced these souls to work for them gathering energy wherever they could.

Ultimately, many of the souls who were forced to work in this way found their way to Earth in the hope that the energy structures in our protected solar system could help prevent the Fourteen devices from working. Unfortunately, this was not the case. Our peculiar energy patterns slowed down the function of the Fourteen devices but they did not stop their energy-gathering functions.

These Fourteen devices are made up of several components. The primary component is an energy-collecting 'crystal' that is located in the abdomen. Energy is drawn into this crystal from any source around the wearer. The collected energy is then transferred into a 'battery pack' located in the small of the back. The battery pack is then connected to a device in the throat, located just below the Adam's apple. When someone of the Fourteen approached anyone fitted with these devices, they would 'plug' into the throat component to discharge the battery pack. There is another component, a mirror image of a Sirian chip, located on the outside of the sacrum bone. This holds an image of the collection of devices and if one or more components are removed, this component will rebuild them.

As a final twist, some souls were also implanted with a miniature copy of the Fourteen implosion devices and these were located in the higher self. Any attempts to remove the implosion device would result in the device using the energy of the two souls, the wearer and the remover, to create a black hole, destroying both souls in the process.

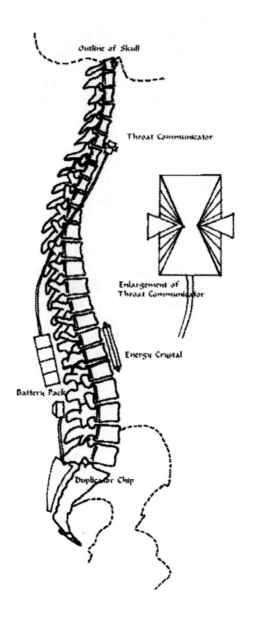

Outline of Skull

Throat Communicator

Enlargement of
Throat Communicator

Energy Crystal

Battery Pack

Duplicator Chip

The main problem generated by having one of these devices implanted, and then taking on human form, is that the function of the thyroid can become severely disrupted and the thyroid reacts as though it has been irradiated. Another 'symptom' of these devices is an innate, sub-conscious, knowledge that a great injustice has been done to your soul and there is then a tendency to want to fight every cause. Some people are also sub-consciously aware that if someone approaches too closely, they will explode.

Since 2002, the Fourteen no longer exist within this Universe and since early 2004, all of their primary energy structures have also been destroyed. With the destruction of these primary energies, these Fourteen energy-gathering devices have begun to dissolve. By the end of 2009, at the latest, these devices will have totally disappeared.

Velon Communicators

Some people took these devices on at the request of the Velon but they had no real idea of what was involved or the implications. Most have been implanted in people without their knowledge or approval. In particular, they have been implanted into those who have primary Atlantean 'Links'.

These devices have six components: five embedded in the abdomen and the main component in the brain.

The abdominal components act like 'batteries' to provide power to the one in the brain. However, they can cause their own problems by producing energy patterns that can act a little like radiation. In particular, the abdominal components can affect the pancreas. The pancreas carries out an amazing number of jobs to keep the body functioning and so disruption to this organ can cause physical problems in many diverse ways. These include: food intolerances, the inability to break down fat in foods, inability to sleep or disrupted sleep

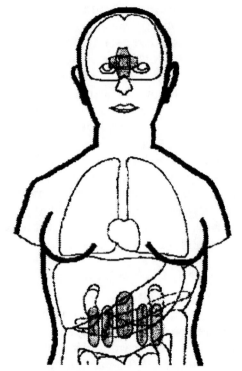

Velon Communicator
as Fitted in Body

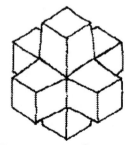

3D Image of Camera

patterns, growths within the body that are non-cancerous or even cancerous growths that have no connection with a particular chakra.

The component embedded in the brain acts like a television camera. If you think of a live television broadcast, this acts in similar ways. Images and sounds, as well as the other senses, are picked up and transmitted live back to Velus. To carry out this function, these devices have an energy potential in the region of five million dimensions. These energy patterns, particularly of this magnitude, can cause severe headaches that are within the brain itself, a pain that is centred just above the junction of the neck and the skull that will not go away no matter how many pain killers are taken.

The Velons were to no longer exist in this Universe beyond the middle of 2005. What was to occur to these communication devices when the Velons left was unclear. Hopefully, they would disappear.

It is only those who are of a semi-physical soul origin that carry these tools. A few, a very few, of the non-physical races do carry the Fourteen structures but they will not carry any of the semi-physical tools as they are incapable of using them in their natural state. Remember, they are only going to be carried by less than one percent of the population so the chances of you having one or more is remote.

If the symptoms described here seem familiar to you, you should consult a healer to see if they can deal with the problems or a kinesiologist who can ask your body directly what it carries and what needs to be cleared.

Psychic Attack

This next section sounds even more far-fetched than the last, unless you have experienced this kind of problem for yourself.

Since the 1950's it has been realised that the mind can be tampered with. It has been found (and practised on many countless occasions) that the mind can be programmed to make the person believe that they are something other than they are. Many assassinations are carried out by people who believe themselves to be an ordinary housewife, factory worker or businessman. By using forms of hypnosis the brain can be programmed to force the person to carry out tasks that, in normal life, they would never consider doing. By programming people in this way military forces the world over have a ready supply of people who can carry out tasks of which they have no conscious knowledge.

The American military, in particular, realised this potential when their soldiers returned from incarceration in Korea 'brain washed' into the communist doctrine of the Koreans. From then on, they have been experimenting with this kind of brain re-programming.

With the Roswell Crash, they realised a new direction of approach that continues to the present day. With the 'alien' crash in New Mexico, they uncovered forms of technology that they had not even dreamt of. What they found were communication systems used by the 'Greys' that could be utilised for 'psychic attack'.

Psychic attack means bending the will of another person by psychically implanting ideas into their mind. This implanting is done from a distance and can be so subtle that the one being manipulated believes they have had a thought that makes them think they should be acting in a particular way, even if the action they are about to take endangers their life and those of others.

All of the 'western' powers have experimented with these types of techniques and varying forms of technology to help enhance an individual's natural psychic capability. The

Chinese, British, North Koreans, Japanese etc have all made use of 'remote' viewing systems either for spying or to influence events at a distance. The Russians, for example, have built their own copies of Grey technology usually made from brass. The Greys do not use these devices as weapons. Their original usage is as communication devices. The small, individual ones were originally used a little like a personal phone as they allowed psychic communication between ships and across distances equivalent to our solar system. The Russian copies of these devices tend to be used by individuals to allow them to target another individual.

The most classic use of these techniques was in the 1970's when the Russians stationed someone in a building opposite the American embassy in Moscow. The Russian operative psychically targeted the American ambassador who was not liked by the Russians and wanted him replaced. To kill him off would have sparked an international incident and so

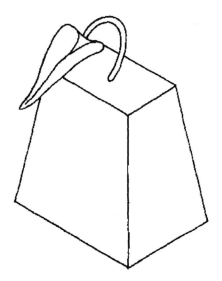

A 'Russian' Psychic Communicator

efforts were made to affect the rhythms of his heart muscles. The Russians were successful enough in their attempts for the ambassador to be sent home on health grounds and a new ambassador appointed.

The 'leaf' component of these devices acts like antennae that allow psychic projections to be finely focused and directed.

The American secret services have also built their own versions of Grey technology although, as their association with the Greys has been much closer than the Russians, the Americans tend to use the Grey devices in their original, semi-physical forms. The Greys have even gone so far as to build devices to the Americans' specifications.

The pyramid device, illustrated below, is an original Grey communicator. Unlike the Russian copies of individual communicators, this device is used as a communication relay system, a little like a telephone exchange on Earth, and is about one thousand times more powerful than the individual ones. They are about 90 cm (3ft) tall and each face of the pyramid is covered with about seventy-six of the 'leaf' antennae as shown on the Russian model. These pyramids can be used either by a number of operatives at the same time to target a large number of people or they can be used by a group of people to generate an accumulation of psychic 'charge' targeted at one individual.

The Grey use of these devices is totally benign, purely as communication systems. In the hands of humans, they have been turned into weapons. These types of weapons are not easily detectable and their effects cannot be seen outside of the mind of the person being attacked in this way.

There are a number of people who claim to be ex CIA remote viewers now offering weekend workshops in remote viewing techniques. Whilst they might sound like a bit of fun most are a cover for recruiting people with a psychic potential above the average. Those who show an aptitude for this kind of work are frequently offered further training, whether in establishments such as GCHQ in Cheltenham or a facility in the States.

Once recruited in this way, it is virtually impossible to leave the 'remote viewing' programme, as you will also have been forced to sign official documents promising not to talk about anything you have learned.

There are also other systems used by the American secret services that have been specifically built for them by the Greys. These are more like electronic machines than

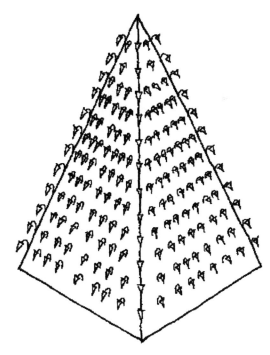

A 'Grey' Communication System

pyramids. They look like large metal cabinets but inside are components in their semi-physical state arranged in patterns like series of printed circuit boards but the boards are composed of energy.

These kinds of devices have two main functions. The first is to record and store personal details of the people they wish to target. The components used to do this look exactly like the Galaxy chip illustrated previously. Each of these chips can store the images, biographical details and energy 'signatures' of up to ten thousand people. Once stored, these details can be called up on to a screen where the operative can then target them with their psychic messages. Each cabinet contains five thousand of these chips, that is the records of, potentially, fifty million people stored in each cabinet. This is the scale of the problem.

They are used to affect the lives of many thousands of people from politicians to dissidents to soldiers to virtually anyone who they think is some kind of threat to them or to national security. There was a law passed in the States in 2004 under the Homeland Security blanket of laws – The Patriot Act - that states that anyone even thinking bad thoughts about America is a criminal and potential terrorist, and should be treated as such. These people are also targets for this kind of psychic attack from the secret services.

The FBI spies on America, the CIA spies on the rest of the world (and quietly on America) whilst the NSA (National Security Agency) spies on the FBI, the CIA and everybody else. The NSA alone has an annual budget that exceeds that of most Third World countries. The American annual budget for its military and secret services is sufficient to keep the world population fed and watered for several years.

Believe it or not, the world is changing for the better; people are regaining their higher levels of consciousness. It is these kinds of ridiculous laws which reflect the fact that people are not looking to the state any longer for answers, they are finding them for themselves. Globally, many countries have passed similar laws to protect themselves from this change of responsibilities. The state is responding by closing in on itself and passing more and more draconian laws to try to protect itself whilst attempting to threaten the personal freedom of individuals to act for themselves. This state of affairs does appear to be a major problem for individuals but all it really shows is a reflection of how much we have already actually achieved in these changes.

Chapter Eleven

Conclusions

We are on the brink of a shift in consciousness so huge that it is hard to comprehend what we will be when we arrive on the other side. Twenty thousand years of searching has arrived at the point where we know what the answers are.

We are finally set to embark on a process of change that has never been attempted before anywhere at any time in the past. We are unique. Nowhere else in the whole of Creation does life at the physical density we live within exist. The Human Experiment has sent ripples of joy and hope throughout this and all of the other Universes.

But, where are we?

As we entered 2005, it was difficult to see anything positive about the year ahead. The invasion of Iraq was continuing to be bloody and no nearer to resolution. So much uranium has been dumped on to the ground that the oil is too contaminated to be used. The United Nations report entitled 'The Silent Genocide' states that so much radiation is present in Iraq and Afghanistan following the use of uranium-coated shells, depleted and live, that there is unlikely to be viable future generations in these countries.

Israel and Palestine are no closer to peace. Several African countries have conflicts that have been raging for twenty years or more, South America is in turmoil and the countries bordering the Indian Ocean have been swamped by a massive tidal wave created by one of the biggest earthquakes ever recorded.

Not very encouraging.

But, if we look beneath the surface, there are reasons for all that has been occurring in the last nine years.

On the fourteenth of August 1996, a new energy was connected to the Earth. This energy triggered virtually all of the subsequent events, individually and globally.

This new energy is more powerful than anything seen since the days of Atlantis and provided an alarm call to wake up humanity from the depths of its slumbers. The connection of this new energy source was programmed into our learning process from the beginning, seven thousand years ago. It was designed to help us remember that we had a job to do and a time limit to that job. We had become so accustomed to being human that we had largely forgotten ourselves and our purpose. This new energy did two things: it awoke us from our slumbers and it asked a question of every single person on the planet – are we ready to return to full consciousness? This question was asked on a higher self level and on a mass consciousness level.

Our reply, individually and collectively, was that sixty per cent of the population did not feel ready for this change. Let us put this answer into context.

For the past seven thousand years we have been investigating, on the Earth's behalf, how to be human, how to fit the whole of the soul into the physical body. This investigation, knowledge-gathering, we have called 'Karma'. Each person planned and lived through a series of lifetimes investigating every single aspect of life on Earth. All of this accumulated information was collected together in a part of the mass consciousness dedicated to keeping a record, the 'Akashic'. Everyone on Earth has had a part to play in this knowledge-gathering process. Some have taken their task extremely seriously and worked diligently in each lifetime. Some have taken their own chosen paths in a way which was a little more relaxed whilst others have just enjoyed the pleasures that the Earth has to offer. Each chose, nobody set us goals, nobody stood over us to ensure that we carried out our tasks. Each person freely chose their path.

There were several times throughout the course of human history when we could have put this accumulated knowledge to its full and final use but, for many reasons, we did not. As we arrived at the year 1900, we began to realise that we were running out of our allotted time and we needed to complete all of the tasks we had set ourselves. This was a century of huge conflict on a global level but it was also the century which finally removed the social shackles we had chained ourselves into. Some embraced this new sense of freedom with an open heart whilst others tried to shut us back into our past.

The First and Second World Wars might have caused a massive loss of physical life but they did allow us to finally liberate ourselves from social hierarchies and Victorian oppressive attitudes. The new personal freedoms gained since World War Two opened up the possibility that our change could occur.

Those who embraced these new freedoms are the ones who began to clear their paths of all of the accumulated debris whilst those who wanted to stay in the past were the ones who felt unable to move onwards. Those who felt unable to complete their chosen paths were the sixty per cent who since 1996 have been gradually returning home to the places of their origin.

With the connection of the new energies in 1996, other questions have also been answered.

Whilst the site of the connection of this new energy source was Britain, it was connected to twelve other energy sites located worldwide. Connecting these thirteen primary energy points is a new 'ley line' network which distributed all of these energies across the globe. These are energies targeted specifically at humans and are designed to help us in our task of completion.

These energies are also intended for use by the planet. As we are changing in our levels of consciousness, so is the Earth. As we expand, so does the Earth expand to match our changing levels of awareness.

Once the new energies were established, other subsequent events could occur. Two days after the primary new connection was made, another connection was established. This was a temporary energy 'bridge' between the Earth and the realms of the Faerie or, more importantly, the Sidhé.

The Sidhé could be described as the 'management' of the Faerie, beings who control the energy patterns around which the Faerie work their magic. These beings were removed from direct connection with the Earth in the year 538 as a means of protecting them from potential harm from man-made religions. They have been able to return periodically to ensure that their work could be continued and the Faerie were kept more or less under control, but they did not have full and free access.

Since 1996, the Sidhé have had full access to the Earth so that they could begin their work to undo the threat that genetically modified organisms (GMO's) present to all of the life on Earth. These GMO's are human constructs but we are unable to protect life from the kind of contamination and irreversible damage of which these modified plants are capable. Neither can we undo the damage once it has occurred. The Sidhé are the only ones capable of undoing this damage. This is why they were brought back earlier than was safe for them; the threat from GMO's was too immediate and too damaging to allow the threat to continue.

Other connections to the Sidhé have subsequently been made that makes their presence now permanent. The threat of GMO's is now lessened but it has not entirely gone. One more major mistake with these GMO's, and their bacterial vectors, and we could still be faced with complete genetic meltdown of all life on the planet. That scenario does not bear thinking about, as it would mean that there would be no viable life on Earth of any kind.

Not content with the potential damage presented by their genetic tinkering, the scientific community is now working with a new threat to life – nano technology. This new technology is the manipulation of living organisms on a molecular level. This is where the molecular structure of a plant is 'adjusted' to new positions and new combinations to make alterations in the way the plant grows and produces its crop.

As with GM, the danger of this form of manipulation is when the plant reproduces. The molecular adjustments can be passed on to the next generation with unknown consequences either for the strain of plant manipulated in this way or for other plants around them when cross pollination occurs. Some of the plants manipulated in this way are already finding their way on to supermarket shelves and there is no labelling to warn of the contents being altered in this way.

With the new energies firmly established and functioning fully, the next point of change occurred on the 31st December 1999. Many saw the turn of the millennium as the point of change whereas it was an accumulation of energetic build-up since 1996 that allowed the frequencies to step up one level.

Those who are working with the new energies felt the shift occur whilst for most it was the new year bringing in change. For many, the change in the man-made calendar provided them with an excuse to make fundamental changes in their lives – the divorce courts very rapidly built up a six-month backlog. For others, it allowed them a marker to bring their lives to an end. The change to 2000 brought with it at least a ten-day waiting list to most crematoriums and cemeteries. This death rate has continued ever since bringing with it a continuing shrinking population. The global population is now one and a half billion less than in 1996.

However, the biggest change that has already been undertaken is with the base frequencies at which all of life exists.

Every living thing on Earth has an energetic resonance with the Earth itself. The first, base, chakra has the same lowest frequency whether a blade of grass, an elephant, a fish or a human. It is this base frequency that connects everything to the Earth. This base 'note' was one of the main reasons why humans had experienced such difficulties and so many problems since our first arrival on Atlantis; the frequency was too low.

The natural resonance of the Earth, the base note frequency, has always been seven point five six (7.56) cycles per second. At the end of May 2000, this base note was altered to three thousand five hundred (3,500) cycles per second.

All of the life on Earth changed in that twenty-four hour period with a great deal of help from the Sidhé and our friends from NGC 584. Every living thing became rejuvenated and regenerated. All natural plants sprang into a new life whilst those that had been weakened by manipulation by mankind began a decline. The increasing failure of, particularly, wheat crops since the summer of 2002 is due to this frequency shift. Wheat has been tampered with so much by man that its energetic and genetic structures could not cope with the shift.

Following the change in this base note frequency, numerous other energy shifts and re-balances have been undertaken. Most of this re-balancing has been aimed at the human template.

The purpose of our change is to make ourselves 'human' again. The planet has allowed us to be 'sub-human' for over seven thousand years and we need to raise ourselves up to refit back into the original human template. Each energy shift has allowed us to make one more step to achieving our goal.

Seven thousand years ago we adopted a 'modified' body form. The soul was divided into two halves and it communicated to us through the chakras which were coloured red, orange, yellow, green, blue, indigo and violet. This pattern of colours, with a few exceptions, continued up to the end of 1996. With the new energies connected, those who had been working towards completing their chosen path began to change the colours of the chakras to the copper golds and petrol blues etc. discussed in an earlier chapter. Gradually, every physical soul changed to these colours. When that point was reached, in 2002, the template was changed to include these intermediary stage colours. Nobody on Earth had the old (red, orange, yellow etc.) colours as we moved into 2003.

What this means is that to come to Earth and take on human form, every soul must adopt these new colours or they will not fit into the human template. If you cannot fit into the template, you cannot take on human form.

Some individuals were so spurred on by this massive shift in energies that they decided to 'complete' their whole pattern of change. On the 2nd of June 2003, sixty-eight people re-fitted themselves into the original, Atlantean, human template. Since then, a further two hundred and fifty thousand people have joined them.

By the end of May 2004, marked by the start of the Venus 'Transit', the template again shifted to the chakras containing no colours at all, just pure soul energy. This placed pressure on people to catch up with their own chosen paths and has resulted in a huge increase in illnesses, such as cancers, as the soul attempts to pass on the message.

The Earth is doing everything she can to work with us and cause as little disruption as possible. She is also undergoing a massive change as she moves with us in our endeavours. Unfortunately, with the increase in diameter of the planet, there comes extreme pressures on the edges of landmasses. Most of these pressures can be released by a minor earth tremor but with so many people trying to prevent earth-quakes occurring, the pressure built to a point where there could have been a series of catastrophic earthquakes and volcanoes. The Earth did not want this situation to occur as it would cause too many problems for all life, particularly to people. All of this pressure, this excess energy, was vented off into space on the 28th of June 2004. Some earthquakes have occurred since then, especially in the Indian Ocean, but they were much smaller and less widespread than they would have been had the Earth not taken this step.

With all of this pressure successfully vented, a full re-evaluation of the situation was undertaken by the Earth, the Thirteen and all of the souls connected with Earth. The restructuring of the Universal energies was more or less complete and the available energies 'quantified'. Our 'contract' with the Earth was to complete our process of change by the end of 2011. Whilst there had been problems over the centuries that were not of human making or even events that could have been predicted, it was agreed by all that this end date must be adhered to. Humanity cannot be given an extension of time beyond the end of 2011 to complete our chosen task. We must regain the original human template or we cannot remain on the planet. Given there were a number of people who had already completed the reintegration process it was felt, by all, that completion by the original end date was not an impossible task.

To help us in our process of completion, the Earth diverted more of her energies into 'charging up' the crystal deposits at many locations around the world. The idea of this was to provide her nurturing energies to help mankind move on.

With a combination of energies and considerable progress already made, the energies were once again adjusted on the 21st of September 2004. The readjustment began, then reached its peak at the end of February 2005. This was a further template shift to no chakras at all. In other words, there must be a sufficient 'quantity' of the soul within the physical where communication from the soul becomes instantaneous.

All that this new situation really does is to help us focus on regions of our lives that still require a little attention. The progression of future events resulting from this new impetus is almost impossible to predict. Each individual will make individual choices and those choices will affect the whole. One thing is clear, the period between the end of 2005 and 2009 is going to be one of turmoil. How tumultuous it turns out to be depends upon our determination to hold to our goal, to hold to our truth.

We are human. We have tried to bring together the immensity of the soul and fit it into the smallness of the human body. We have not realised how small we have become. We see the body as somehow, somewhere, having a soul, an eternal consciousness. We have forgotten that we are that soul and that the body is just a function along our route to becoming human.

All times of change bring with them uncomfortable readjustments. Our readjustment is to remember that we have deliberately placed ourselves into a situation where we had the ability to change the whole of Creation. In our confinement, we have learned to be small and have lost our place within the whole. Waking up to reality is proving to be a painful exercise. Each step we take brings new realities to light and that increases the pressure, increases the pain. We were not unprepared for this. We knew when we began our journey that claiming our goal was not going to be easy. As human history, human development, unfolded each step took us closer but also further away from our true beings. We have always been pulled in several directions at once and each choice we made at these points of conflict either took us closer to or further away from our true selves. At times it was easier to go 'with the flow' whilst at others it was better to fight for who we are. All adding to our sum of knowledge. All adding to us, personally and collectively.

We know the answers. At long, oh so long last, we know the answers. But, do we have the final piece of courage to put the answers into action?

yes, with a small 'y'. Nobody is shouting 'we have won', nobody is shouting at all. There is a sigh, no more than that. A job well done requires no more.

But where do we go from here? What further steps do we need to take and are there further problems still to be encountered? We, humanity, are a part of a Universal whole, a Universal Soul. We are not alone in our struggles. Every single soul within this universe is working with us as much as they possibly can. But they cannot intervene directly. WE set ourselves our task and it is WE who want to complete it on our own. This is OUR choice. Collectively and individually we all wanted to see the job through by ourselves and for ourselves so where we go next is also our decision.

For many of those who have worked hard on completing their chosen path, there can be a sense of confusion. If I have done it, why hasn't everyone else? Where is this change? The answers lie within. If you take a look back at your lives you will see that the years since 1996 have been ones of immense change, personally and globally. The whole population has made many steps out of the past, in particular, steps away from the control of others. Some have stepped a long way whilst others not so far. The real differences between one group and another is that of courage, the courage to make changes in their lives.

One step creates the biggest change of all, being honest. Honest with yourself and honest with those you share your life with. This is the direction we all need to go in order to complete the process of change – total honesty in all aspects of our lives.

This step to honesty is the one which is the key to everything else. The more honest we are with each other, the more we free up all of the energies needed to complete our chosen paths.

Honesty means saying what you feel about a situation. If you want to do something, say so. If you do not want to do something, say so. If someone else's actions have upset you, say so. If you disagree with something, say so. An expression of true honesty is all that is required. This is the courage that all of those making this change have found, the courage to be honest and take the consequences. As each person becomes more honest in their lives, it gives permission for those around them to be honest in return. This cycle of honest response unlocks everything and releases all of us to complete our future. Conflicts only arise, personally or globally, because of a lack of honesty. If there is total honesty, there is no conflict.

Recognition of the rare times when total honesty would be inappropriate is becoming second nature - as intuition increases, so does the recognition of when it is best not to be totally honest, for these occasions it is best to be discreet and use the 'Giveaway' (see appendix).

This is what makes the predicting of future events so difficult. The more honest we become, the easier life becomes. The more we hold on to our old ways, our old masks, the more the soul pushes us to clear them. The more we resist the soul, the more conflict arises. If we all became totally honest tomorrow, we would all complete our reintegration the day after.

This is the answer to all of the questions, if we all embrace our own truths and express those truths honestly, there will be no conflict and our transitions will be smooth and simple. If we resist our truths, fight against our souls, there will be conflict and there will be a struggle to finish our transitions at all.

We are completing a search for answers we began twenty thousand years ago. The last seven thousand of those years have been an intensive search. It is time to now take full control of our collective destiny and put our accumulated knowledge into full use.

We have already taken most of the steps needed to complete our plans. There is only one final step left and the path to that final step is paved with the truth.

"............I see in your eyes the same fear that would take the heart of me. The day may come when the courage of men fails - when we forsake our friends and break all bonds of fellowship. But it is not this day.
An hour of wolves and shattered shields, when the age of men comes crashing down.
But it is not this day.
This day we fight.
By all that you hold dear on this good Earth – I bid you stand".

Speech to his troops by Aragorn at the start of the final battle to take Mordor.

Words spoken by the actor Viggo Mortensen from the film version of JRR Tolkien's book 'The Return of the King' by Peter Jackson and Wingnut Films.

See author's note.

Author's Note

I have chosen to use quotations from the film version of JRR Tolkien's *Lord of the Rings* trilogy for the frontispiece and endpiece as they perfectly sum up the mood of our times. The three films are produced by Wingnut Films and directed by Peter Jackson.

Tolkien's books were written in the 1930's at a time when we were poised to undergo the current changes. We failed at that time, for a number of reasons, but the books reflected what was beginning to occur and they fit perfectly into the current time.

The start of the story, *The Fellowship of the Ring* reflects the period from 1996 to 2005 where we began to wake up to the realities that we needed to take matters in hand to achieve a goal we were not too sure of. The second book, *The Two Towers*, can be likened to the period between 2005 and 2009 where there is conflict and turmoil as those who are seeking change confront those who would oppose. The final book, *The Return of the King*, is likely to be the period of late 2009 to early 2010 where the conflict comes to its end. This ending begins a new phase where choices undreamed of prior to this date now present themselves.

The quote on the frontispiece is from the end of the battle for Osgiliath where events could turn away from the success of the 'Fellowship'. The two characters; Frodo Baggins and Samwise Gamgie, now realise that only part of their task has been fulfilled and there are many other dangers to come.
This reflects the potential events possible between 2005 and

2009 – a completion of some aspects of the task bring a sharper focus on what is left to be done.

The quote at the end could be the end of this four-year period. Many battles have been fought and won and the thought of yet another fight disheartens the men of the armies. Aragorn's speech is made at a time where the armies stand outside the gates of Mordor and they realise the horror that lies behind. As the battle rages, Frodo and Sam complete their tasks and the armies of Mordor collapse and scatter.

Frodo and Sam are little people, Hobbits, who undertake the largest and most arduous task of the story reflecting that no matter how small you think you might be, you can take a major role in the changes to come.

Aragorn's speech is included here as many have a sense of foreboding of what is happening and what is to come – unknown dangers always appear to bring about the most disquiet. Really, we need to focus on the task in hand. Instead of attempting things that are already being taken care of, such as earthquakes, we need to focus on the problems that are just under the surface.

Whilst it is not possible to predict the timing of future events, the substance of the events can be.

The first change we are likely to see is the realisation that the terrorist threat epitomised by 'Al Qaeda' are not genuine. Whilst there are 'terrorist' groups operating in various locations around the world, there is no global terrorist network, Al Qaeda or otherwise. Terrorist groups only form when their way of life or beliefs are threatened by an invading force. If Britain had been invaded in WW2, the British would have formed groups who chose to fight against the occupying forces. In other words, they would have become terrorists.
It is not possible to predict how long the sham of Al Qaeda

will be maintained by various governments, but they do have other imaginary threats already in the pipeline. A fearful population is one that is easily manipulated and this is the reason for a succession of frightening scenarios likely to be brought in to the public eye over the next few years.

Following on from international terrorists will be a threat from space. As mentioned in a previous chapter, there are many thousands of lumps of rock floating around in space many of which are big enough to wipe out life on Earth. Bringing this into public understanding will enable the western governments to gain support for putting weapons into space. The claim being that the weapons will be pointed outwards, away from the Earth, in order to destroy any meteorites that stray too close. Space is currently, officially in anyway, free of any kinds of weapons but there are several governments who would like public approval for weapons to be placed there so that they can used against ground based forces.

The Earth already has her own defence system against meteorites, as witnessed in Tunguska in 1908. We do not need weapons in space for any reason.

Once space has been weaponised, the following threat will be from extra terrestrial races. We all know from many Fifties science fiction movies that all extra terrestrial beings are very unpleasant and always want to rule the world taking great pleasure in destroying as many humans as possible.

There are thirteen races with which we share our Universe. Six of them, the non-physical races, comprise something like ninety eight per cent of the souls who are in human form. As they are non-physical, they cannot use any kind of 'tool' let alone weapon. The semi-physical races do use tools but none of them, not one, have developed any kind of 'weapon'. The only race that posed a threat to Earth were the Velons and this race will have left the Universe by the middle of 2005. There is nobody 'out there' who is a threat to human existence or to the life on Earth.

Whilst these items are likely to be heralded by a great deal of political publicity, the real threats go unchallenged if not unnoticed.

GMO's and nano technology have been discussed earlier but there are other, more immediate threats, which are increasing.

Although they are not a legal requirement (not yet), there is huge pressure on parents to have their children vaccinated. There are currently something like twenty vaccines recommended by western governments to be administered to all children before the age of sixteen. Ignoring the obvious problems of live or dead viruses and the effectiveness of these vaccines in the first place, the real problem arises from the way in which preservatives are added to them (source: Nexus Magazine).

All vaccines, whether the live or dead forms, have a short life-span and so preservatives are added to them to ensure that there are always supplies ready for use. The preservatives used are manufactured either from a form of aluminium or a form of mercury. Both of these substances attack the central nervous system and both of these substances can be absorbed into brain tissue. These substances are injected into children as young as three months when their brains and nerve structures are not fully formed. It is these substances, the vaccine preservatives, that are responsible for VCJD in humans and BSE in cattle. The BSE epidemic had nothing to do with contaminated feed, it was the aluminium derivative used to preserve veterinary vaccines that was the cause. This is why the law requires that the nerve and brain tissue of animals is not allowed to enter the human food chain.

Added to which, the chemicals added to drinking water under the name of 'Fluoride' are also aluminium derivatives.

In recent years we have seen an inordinate rise of problems with the central nervous system and moods of children – there can be very little doubt that these metal derivatives are responsible.

Given the rise of perceived behavioural problems in children, the medics have come up with new names to describe them, the two most common are ADD and ADHD. These illnesses do not actually exist in the terms under which the medics describe health problems. However, there is a massive rise in the rate of diagnosis made in these names. Consequential with this rise in diagnosis is the rise of the number of drugs prescribed to treat these doubtful diagnoses. The drugs prescribed to treat ADD and ADHD are known as psycho-tropic drugs. These drugs are a cocaine derivative that turn children into 'zombies'. Even if your child survives the effects of the drugs, many come off their medication as cocaine addicts.

These are the real issues that need to be fought. The Earth is well able to look after herself and protect the life in her nurture whilst doing so. What we need to do is to get on with the job of being us, being human, and not worry about the aspirations of politicians. Let's face it, if you aspire to being a politician, you have many ambitions of holding power and these ambitions leave you open to the influences of vested interests. For a long time, it has been clear that these vested interests want control and will try to gain that control without regard to human life. Whether that control is to do with wealth or the bringing about of Armageddon is immaterial. It is this desire for control where most of our coming battles will be fought.

There is a reality out there that is not reported in most newspapers. To find it I would suggest a balanced reading of 'Nexus' magazine and the newspaper 'Positive News'. Between these two publications there is at least truth.

Chris Thomas

www.psychic-surgery.co.uk

Appendix One

Some Helpful Exercises

The following are some exercises which many have found useful.

The Giveaway

This is a process of 'giving away' emotions to paper, releasing them from the body. This exercise can be used for past traumatic events or can be used for events that occurred today. The originator of the emotions can be either alive or dead, it makes no difference - what you are doing is clearing the emotions out of your system.

If you have been in a situation where you wanted to express yourself honestly but for whatever reason felt that you could not or there have been instances in your past, even from childhood, where there have been situations where you felt prevented from expressing yourself properly or fully, this tool will help to release the emotions of these situations that you are still carrying around with you.

If there is a person you can identify with a particular situation, such as a parent, relative, boss, etc. write them a letter saying to them exactly what you would have wanted to say but, for whatever reason, you felt you could not. DO NOT READ IT BACK - this is the important bit. Just rip it up and dispose of it, preferably by burning.

The same applies to day to day situations - supermarket queues, broken pipes, flat tyres, your boss, your landlord, traffic queues, etc. etc. when you get home, you can write to these situations or people.

The giveaway process is effective at clearing your past problems as well as day to day situations which have made you feel angry or frustrated but felt unable to express your feelings fully and honestly. It sounds too simple a tool to work - until you try it. Once the giveaway is used, you will be surprised just how powerful a tool it can be.

The best way of dealing with emotional situations is to be as honest as possible in your expression of how you feel as the situation arises; if it is not possible to do so, use the giveaway as soon as possible.

It might be necessary to use the giveaway more than once to any particular situation or event. If you have done your giveaway and the emotion of the event still surfaces, use the giveaway again, or several times more, until you feel totally clear of the emotions. If the person is still alive and the situation still 'niggles', you will eventually have to deal with them direct as your higher self is continuing to try and help you to be totally honest!

This change we are undergoing does produce some strange effects both within ourselves and within those with whom we share our lives. Those who are changing often find that those around them no longer understand them and can attack them on many levels. You can also experience strange energy depletions just by walking down the street or by visiting friends in hospital.

The following exercises are designed to help alleviate some, if not all, of these kinds of problems.

There are three meditations. One is designed to boost your energies as high as they will go or to repair energy depletion when it occurs. One is designed to help you make closer and sustainable contact with a 'spirit guide' and the last helps you to take a look at any issues that are outstanding and you might have overlooked whilst at the same time reinforcing your connection with your higher self.

The last two exercises are intended to be shielding devices. The first to help you survive your daily life the second to guard against any psychic attack problems you might be experiencing.

Meðitation One
Chakra Balancing Meðitation

This exercise is probably the most important of all as it re-balances and re-energises your whole system. It can be used at any time, anywhere, and only takes about ten to fifteen minutes to complete. We are going to be using completely transparent energy. This is like a hot summer's day when the heat is rising in shimmers from the ground: this is what transparent energy looks like, a heat haze shimmer. This meditation can be used no matter what stage you are at in the process of change. If your chakras are still of the 'intermediary' colours, this will help boost your system and help you move on. This exercise can even be used if you have no chakras at all as it will put the right kind of energy into the correct places on the spine. It does not matter which direction the chakras spin in, just allow them their natural flow.

Start by sitting or lying quietly. Begin to concentrate on your breath. Breathe in and breathe out, just focus on your breath. As you breathe in and breathe out, you start to relax. Start with the bottom of your feet. Each breath relaxes the bottom of your feet. Then your calves begin to relax with each breath followed by your thighs, your buttocks, your lower back, middle back and, finally, your shoulders and neck. Each breath relaxing and cleansing.

As you relax, begin to form a point of concentration about one foot (30cm) above the top of your head. Once you feel your concentration has begun to form a small ball, bring that point of concentration all of the way down the spine down to the first (root) chakra. When you have reached the very bottom of your coccyx, form a cone of energy made from the heat haze shimmer with the point of the cone attached to the bottom of the coccyx and the cone opening directly downwards in a direct line with your spine. Concentrate on this vortex, this cone of pure energy, for a couple of minutes. Feel the energy of the cone spin very quickly. The faster the spin, the further the cone extends downwards. Faster and faster it spins, further and further the cone of energy extends.

Now move up to the second chakra, just where the spine and the pelvis meet.

This time, the vortex forms equally front and back of the body. The point of the transparent vortex is connected to the spine and the cones opening equally front and back. As the vortices begin to spin, they become clearer and clearer. Once you have the transparent vortices spinning as fast as you can imagine, move on to the next chakra.

The third chakra is located in the small of the back, just above where the tummy button is. Again, the vortices open equally front and back with the point of the cone connected to the spine. Imagine them spinning. As they spin, they become clearer and clearer. Once you have the transparent vortices spinning as fast as you can imagine, move on to the next chakra.

The fourth chakra is located where the heart is. The points of the transparent vortices are connected to the spine and open equally front and back. As you make the vortices spin, they become clearer and clearer. Once you have the transparent vortices spinning as fast as you can imagine, move onto the next chakra.

The fifth chakra is located in the throat, between the Adam's apple and the chin. The points of the vortices are connected to the spine and open equally front and back. As the vortices begin to spin, they become clearer and clearer. Once you have the transparent vortices spinning as fast as you can imagine, move on to the next chakra.

The sixth chakra is located just above the bridge of the nose on a line where the spine would be if it continued up through the head. The vortices connect to this imaginary line and open equally front and back. Make the transparent vortices spin and as they spin, they become clearer and clearer. Once you have the transparent vortices spinning as fast as you can imagine, move on to the next chakra.

The seventh chakra is located on the top of the head, in a direct line with the spine. The point of the vortex is connected to the top of the head and the cone opens directly upwards in a line with the spine. Again, make this spin as fast as you can. The faster it spins, the clearer it becomes. Once you have it spinning as fast as you can imagine, begin to extend the point of the vortex down through the head connecting it into the sixth chakra. Now bring it further down connecting into the fifth chakra, the fourth chakra, the third chakra, the second chakra and finally all the way down to connect into the first chakra.

As it connects with the first chakra, you whole system comes into balance. Balanced and fully energised. At this point, you can take one of two steps. You can use this point of balance and energising to move on to one of the other meditations or you can complete the exercise as follows.

Once you have connected to the first chakra and your system has become fully energised, bring your point of concentration back up the spine to just above the top of your head and slowly, slowly bring yourself back into the present.

Please note. There is no need to 'shut down' once this meditation has been completed. That concept is a Victorian hangover that is not relevant. By fully energising and balancing the chakras in this way, your system is as powerful and protected as it can be. If you consciously 'shut down' you will undo all of the work and deplete your system.

Meditation Two
Guide Meditation

Begin with the chakra-balancing meditation. Once you have completed the full sequence of the meditation, bring the point of concentration back to just above the top of your head.

You are in a garden. The sun is shining and the sky is clear blue. It is warm but not hot, comfortable. Around you are trees and flowers. Everywhere is green and pleasant, warm and comfortable. There are flowers that have a brightness of colour that catches the breath. Their perfume reaches you on a gentle breeze. The birds are singing and there is a gentle buzz of insects. Everywhere is comfortable, everything is harmony.

Just stand for a moment and take in the sensations of harmony, the colours, the sounds and the perfumes. Peace and harmony.

As you look around you realise you are standing on a path. It is not very well defined in the grass, but you are able to follow it easily with your eyes.

Slowly, you begin to walk straight ahead on this little path. Just slowly taking in the sights and smells of your special little garden. And, as you slowly walk up the slight slope of the path, you realise that this is your garden, it belongs only to you. You are free and relaxed. As you walk up your little path you can take in the sights, sounds and smells and become one with your garden. Comfortable and in harmony. This is your garden and you are free to visit any time you wish. All you need to do is relax and you can be in your special garden.

As you slowly walk up your little path you realise that the path turns a little towards the right, just behind a flowering bush. As you come around the bend, you take in the musky perfume of the bush and, just for a moment, enjoy the change of view.

The path turns to the left and begins a gentle slope downwards. As you begin to walk slowly down the path you can see ahead of you a little wooden bridge over a gently sparkling stream. The bridge is gently shaded by a couple of tall trees that allow you to see the little stream as it sparkles under the bridge.

As you lift your eyes a little you can see that there is a little seat on the other side of the bridge. On the seat a figure is seated and, as you cross the little bridge, the figure rises and comes to stand by your side.

You are not sure whether you know this person but they are somehow familiar and you feel very comfortable in their presence.

As you continue your journey, your new companion begins to walk along with you. As you walk, you can ask your companion any question that comes to mind, anything that you wish to know with the sure knowledge that your question will be answered.

Slowly, bring your concentration back to a point just above the top of your head with the full knowledge that you can visit your garden any time you wish and that your new friend will be there to answer any questions you wish. Slowly, bring yourself back into the present and open your eyes feeling relaxed, refreshed and fully balanced and energised.

Meditation Three
Higher Self Meditation

Begin with the chakra balancing meditation. Once you have completed the full sequence of the meditation, bring your point of concentration back to just above the top of your head.

You are on the side of a mountain, very near the top and just climbing on to an open area, like a small plateau. The air is clear and fresh and you feel healthy and invigorated by the climb. You are comfortably warm but not hot and you are breathing easily after your climb.

As you step on to the plateau you see lots of bushes with large silver flowers and as you breathe in the musky perfume of these flowers, you feel a sense of achievement – you have at last reached the higher ground. You can turn back and look down at your climb and see that all of your struggles, exertions and fights are now far behind you. You no longer need to climb – you have arrived. As you look back on your climb, you can look to see if there are any areas of your life which you have neglected and require you to spend some time to finally clear out.

Do not be afraid of these unresolved areas.

Remember, you are looking at your life and these are a part of you that need a little effort to finally clear out. Do not ignore them. Remember them and know that these small items are all that need to be resolved. All else has been cleared.

As you turn back to the plateau you realise that your vision has changed. It is as if a mist, a veil, has cleared and you can see the peaks of other mountains around you and that they are all below you. You feel your sense of achievement, you have arrived and your world is changed because of your climb. You find a comfortable spot to sit down and enjoy this feeling of completion. Just savour that feeling for a moment. No more climbing to do, all you need to do now is just to be.

As you sit and relax, you become aware of an energy. It is as though you are being showered in a transparent sparkly light from a little way above you. As you become more aware of this energy, you become aware of a mind within it. A mind that is sharing itself directly with your mind and you acknowledge that this mind is somehow closely connected with you. A part of yourself that is familiar but somehow larger than you.

As this higher mind comes closer to you, connections begin to be made directly between one mind and the other. You become aware of the long cords that have always connected the two minds together and that they are becoming shorter and stronger and you feel that both minds are beginning to merge into your mind.

You can feel yourself expanding. Your awareness fills a new larger space and you can see and sense the world in newer and fresher ways. You feel that you can at last understand yourself and your world. You feel that you can at last understand yourself and your world in new ways and with a new light of understanding.

We slowly, slowly return to your point of concentration just above your head with the sure knowledge that this expanded mind of yours is firmly in place and fully connected, never again to be separate. Remember what you saw as you looked down from the mountain and resolve to clear those issues.

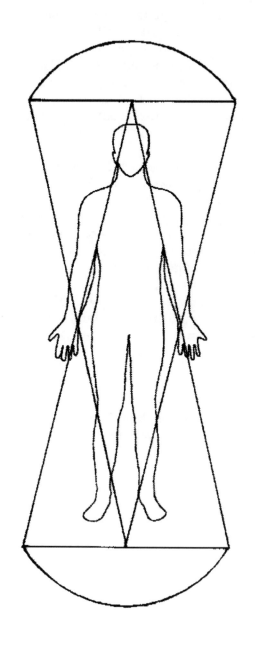

Slowly return into the present feeling relaxed, refreshed and fully balanced.

Protection Shield

As more people progress through their changes, the gap between those who are changing and those who are standing still becomes more and more obvious. Those who are progressing can look a little like a five course dinner, in energy terms, to those who are lagging behind. This shield is designed to do two things. Firstly it protects your energies from being scavenged by those who are not moving forwards: secondly, it provides a disguise to your energies so that you do not stand out so much from the crowd. The difference between people is becoming so marked that we have arrived at the point where this shield has to be worn at all times and only taken down at times where you feel 'safe' and comfortable. Once you have built it the first time, you will only need to think the shield in place in future. You will also need to reinforce it in place from time to time during the day, especially if you come into contact with a lot of people or if you work in a stressful job.

Some people like to give of their energies to others. This is not necessarily a bad thing but it can leave you feeling very depleted at the end of a day. You can still give out if you wish, but you can also protect your own energies at the same time by building the shield and then building an extra 'wall' of transparent energies outside of the shield. Those who are needy can take from the 'wall' but leave your shield intact. You can rebuild your extra energy 'wall' as often as you like during the day.

To build the shield

It is built from the transparent, heat haze shimmery energy we used in the meditations. Start in a standing position with

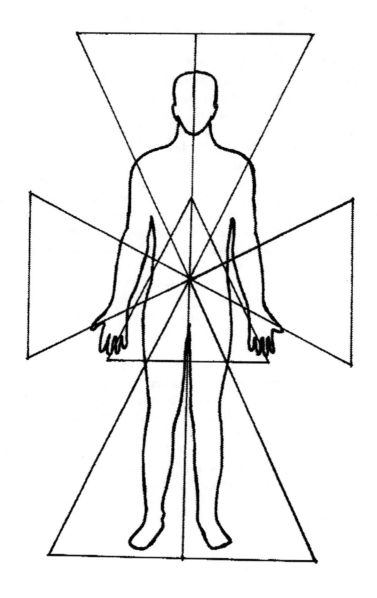

your feet together. Imagine a point about one foot (30cm) below your feet. From this point form a vortex of totally transparent energy with the vortex opening to finish above your head. The point of the vortex is beneath your feet but the cone opens as you build up the body. The open cone of the vortex finishes at about one foot (30cm) above the top of your head and is about three feet (90cm) in diameter.

Next, imagine a point about one foot (30cm) above the top of your head in the centre of the top of the open cone you built from beneath your feet. This vortex opens in the opposite way to the first so that the open end of the transparent cone finishes in a circle around the point of the first vortex. The bottom open end of the cone is again about three feet (90cm) diameter.

Finally, cap the top of the cone above your head with a dome of energy and cap the cone of energy beneath your feet with a dome of energy so that the whole shield looks like the one in the drawing.

Now that you have built the shield once, you do not need to go through the whole exercise again. Just think the shield in place and your higher self will automatically build it for you.

Psychic Protection Shield

Unlike the first shield, this one should be used very sparingly and only in an 'emergency'. The idea of this shield is to protect against a psychic attack but the shield is so powerful that it can cut off communication from your higher self if left in place for too long. If you feel that you are coming under some kind of psychic attack, build this shield immediately but take it down again after a maximum of ten minutes. If you still feel under attack, rebuild it but, generally speaking, the idiots who attempt these kinds of attacks on others give up if they are blocked.

Again, this shield is made from the shimmery transparent energy that the chakras have become and was used in the meditations.

This sounds a very complicated process but it is more complicated to describe than it is to build in practise. The main component of this shield is a three-sided pyramid so you need to practise visualising how one looks. Start by imagining a triangle with equal length sides with each side about three feet (90cm) long. Next, imagine a point about three feet (90cm) above the centre of the triangle. Now imagine lines of clear energy connecting from the points of the triangle to the apex, the point above the middle. This is a three-sided pyramid.

Start in a standing position. Imagine that you are standing in the middle of the pyramid you just built, with the apex positioned at your tummy button. Next, imagine a second-three sided pyramid, identical to the first, but a mirror image with the base triangle central over your head with the apex of this pyramid meeting the apex of the first pyramid at your tummy button.

Now, imagine a pyramid on its side directly in front of you with the apex point meeting the apex points of the first two pyramids at your tummy button. The next pyramid is also on its side but directly behind you again with the apex point meeting the other pyramid apex points at your tummy button.

Now imagine another pyramid on its side, this time coming in on your left hand side with the apex point meeting the other apex points at your tummy button. The sixth and final pyramid is also on its side and on your right with its apex point meeting all of the other apex points at your tummy button.

It sounds extremely complicated when it is described but once you start to build the pyramids you will find that it is straightforward. It is just six three-sided pyramids with their apex points meeting at your tummy button. You might need to practise a few times, though, until you get it right.

Once you have built the structure and it looks like the one in the drawing, make it spin in the vertical axis, around the line of your spine. It does not matter which direction it spins in, just allow it to spin in the way that comes naturally, just make it spin as fast as you can imagine.

Now that you have built it once, you will not need to go through the whole procedure again. If you feel you are coming under psychic attack, just think the shape in place and make it spin, your higher self will be working with you. Try to remember to take it down in as short a time-frame as possible as it is powerful enough to affect communication between you and your higher self.

Appendix Two

Chronological Chart

14,376,279,386 years ago	Creation of the Universal envelope
100 million years ago	Creation of the six non-physical races
40 million years ago	Completion of our solar system with early life forms developing on the outer planets
30 million years ago	Creation of the seven semi-physical races
25 million years ago	Beginnings of life on Earth (Earth's choice to wait)
20 million years ago	Creation of the Sidhé and the Faerie
4.5 million years ago	Neanderthal Man developed by Earth from the early primate models
4 million years ago	The arrival of 'Merlin' on Earth

3.9 million years ago	Removal of four planets from the solar system
3.8 million years ago	Arrival of Cro Magnon Man's template from Mars
3.6 million years ago	Fourteenth Faction burst into this Universe

---

94-98 thousand years ago	Period when Lemuria was established
85 thousand years ago	Atlantis established
65 thousand years ago	Atlantis destroyed
65 thousand years ago	Construction of the Sphinx in Egypt
28 thousand years ago	New energy matrix established to support human life
20 thousand years ago	Human resettlement of the planet begun
18 thousand years ago	Building of the pyramid complex in Egypt
17 thousand years ago	Building of Teotehuacan
12 thousand years ago	First use of language in the form of 'Hebrewa'

| 10 thousand years ago | Construction of Silbury Hill, the Avebury stone circles and the Stonehenge circles |
| 7 thousand years ago | Beginnings of our knowledge gathering process – Karma |

August 14th 1996	Connection of new energy grid to north Devon and the twelve other primary energy points world-wide. First census taken of human readiness for completion
August 16th 1996	Temporary bridge between 'Avalon' to Glastonbury Tor to reconnect the Sidhé to the planet's energies to allow them to begin countering the threat of GMO's
December 31st 1999	Start of the acceleration of the human energy structures allowing further choice and actions based on those choices. Energies reached their peak at the end of May 2002. With this peak, the process of change became unstoppable and could not be reversed
30th May 2000	Earth alters her basic energy patterns from 7.56 Hz to 3,500 Hz. The Sidhé, with the help of the NGC altered all of Earth life

	forms to accommodate this change.
June 2002 to Jan 19th 2004	Various alterations to human template energies and the re-balancing of pressures for human change
June 2nd 2003	First people to complete the whole reintegration process. 25 in America and 43 in Europe completed
January 19th 2004	Human template modified to transparent chakras increasing the pressure to resolve personal issues
May 2004	Further energy structures connected to the Earth to accelerate progress. The Venus transit marked the end of the connection
June 28th 2004	Earth vented off considerable internal pressure from earth-quakes not being allowed to happen by human interference
1st August 2004	Earth confirms that the original Atlantean human template is the only acceptable human form. No other versions will be allowed to remain on the planet after 2011

2nd August 2004	Earth charges up all global crystal deposits. Earth's expansion in size accelerated. Confirmation of arrival of entirely new First Born souls to tribal locations
6th September 2004	Earth time – not Universal time – full removal of Velon race begun. Start of final acceleration of human energies
February 2005	Completion of energy build-up began in September. This energy now holds its peak pressure to bring about the completion of all clearances on an individual and global level. Final census of numbers ready to make the re-integration process. The beginnings of the accelerated removal of those electing not to complete
December 2005 to September 2009	Final choices and final clearances begun leading to a potential period of massive re-adjustments on a global scale. By the end of this period, all human choices will have been fulfilled
September 2009 to March 2010	A period of readjustment for those remaining on the planet as well as the beginnings of mass completions

March 2010 onwards	Your guess is as good as mine. One thing is for certain – it will not be as tumultuous as the previous four years. This is the time for full completion and everything becomes renewed. All possible possibilities become fully open to a future we can design for ourselves – with the help of the planet, the Sidhé and the First Born!

Hopefully, I will see you there.

Other titles by Chris Thomas:

The Journey Home Chris Thomas

Who are we? Why are we here? Are we alone? What relationship does Earth and its multitude of lifeforms have to themselves and to the universe? The answers to many of these questions have long been available, but over the centuries they have become hidden by personal interests and clouded by repetition and dogma. As we undergo a vast shift in consciousness, the underlying reasons for our existence have to be rediscovered and put into their proper perspective. This book brings these issues into a sharper focus and sheds light into some of the darker corners. Gone are the dark days of Karmic re-cycling and suffering; we have reached the time of the birth of a new human existence so far removed from human experience that most have not yet recognised its coming. ISBN 186163 041 7   £7.95

The Fool's First Steps Chris Thomas

"much that makes sense...on a deeper level" Prediction

Are you asking Questions? Transforming? Wanting to know the purpose of it all? Do the old answers no longer work?   The true purposes of Avebury and Stonehenge and the knowledge contained there, stellar gateways, the origins of crop circles, changing Earth energies, the true nature of angels... Personal transformations happening now on a grand scale, mental, emotional and physical. Realising the spiritual origins of the human race... If this book were a novel it would make fascinating reading, but as the explanations again and again strike a true chord, it makes compulsive and unforgettable reading which will help you change how you view life. ISBN 186163 072 7   £9.95

Planet Earth - The Universe's Experiment Chris Thomas

Who are we? Where do we come from? What is our purpose and why did we go wrong? Humans are not of the Earth but have arrived on this planet to explore. On our joyous arrival we encountered the spirits of the land, the Sidhe and the faerie. As we became more human we began to lose our memories of our origins and the knowledge of our true purpose and potential. As we approach the completion of our climb back to reality, we are awakening the ghosts of this knowledge. Lemuria, Atlantis, the thirteen races have all played their part in "The Human Plan", all are now working to assist us to our chosen goal - full consciousness. But, time is short and unless we complete our journey soon, the Earth will be lost to us. Virtually all our experience and history is at odds with the archaeological and scientific versions of our past, only the Akashic tells the real history. What is told here is the Akashic's story. ISBN 186163 224X   £11.95

The Healing Book Chris Thomas & Diane Baker

"The exercises are well described and arranged in a good order of development, clearly relevant case examples..a good basic book written in plain English by two clearly competent healers keen on sharing their knowledge" Touchstone

This book is for those who wish to heal, starting at the beginning of the healing process with simple, easily followed exercises which can begin to unlock the healing potential which is inherent in all of us. Nobody needs to feel left out of these abilities. We are all healers, all that we need to do is to stop telling ourselves that we are not. Whatever level of experience you have of healing, this book explains in simple uncomplicated language that does not use mysticism or any form of ritual, how to understand the "Chakras" and the way in which our daily lives influence them, to relate medical conditions to the chakras and to learn methods which will bring the chakras back into balance, both for yourself and for others. These methods apply equally to humans and to animals. If you do not have any experience of giving healing, but would like to learn, this book can set you on that path. If you already work as a healer, in whatever capacity, and would like to explore your greater potential, this book is also for you. The authors have a combined experience of over twenty five years of providing healing and have taught very many people to unlock their own healing potential. This book is not only about learning to heal from the beginning, but also explores some of the energy manipulation techniques used by the authors in their daily practise as "Psychic Surgeons". ISBN 186163 053 0   £8.95

Everything You Always Wanted To Know About Your Body, But, So Far, Nobody's Been Able To Tell You
Chris Thomas & Diane Baker
"...easy to understand...insight into how you can heal yourself...comprehensive guide" Here's Health

Have you ever wondered why some people become ill and others do not? Why some people recover from illness and others do not? Do you know how your body really works? Why do diets rarely work? Is there an alternative approach to treating symptoms of illness instead of using prescriptive drugs? Well here is a book which leads you through the body, organ by organ, system by system, and explains in clear language how illness arises and what to do about it. It explains the workings of the human body in simple language and clear illustrations; which elements are connected together and why they can influence each other. It also relates each region and organ to its associated chakra and how our day-to-day lives have an influence on our health and well-being. Every part of the body is dealt with in these ways and the major underlying causes for most of our illnesses explained. It also provides details and suggestions on how to heal yourself by working on the root cause issues. This book also takes a look at how some illnesses are brought about by past life traumas and looks at ways of healing the symptoms of illness without the need for prescriptive drugs. Several forms of healing practices are used to achieve this: Bach Flower Remedies, Reflexology, Herbalism, Biochemic Tissue Salts and Homeopathy are the main approaches used, with a further twenty seven therapies fully described. This is an extensive, comprehensive look at the body and illness. It is also one of the most comprehensive guides to alternative treatments currently available. ISBN 186163 0980   £17.95

The Sequel to Everything - The Case Histories
Chris Thomas and Diane Baker
The publication of 'Everything You Always Wanted To Know About Your Body, But, So Far, Nobody's Been Able To Tell You' generated a great deal of interest in a new way of looking at the body and how illness is generated. The authors had many requests for a collection of real case histories to help people understand how the symptoms can be read and how to make more sense of the body and soul's messages. All that is required is an alteration in focus and understanding of the workings of the body and the way in which the soul, the unconscious and the body are inextricably linked together. The book describes the ways in which the symptoms of an illness can be tracked back to its root cause and the "homework" given to help deal with these root cause issues. Illness is not a punishment of any kind, from any source, nor is it a 'test', or an obstacle to be struggled against. Illness is a message from our own soul trying to tell us that we have taken a step in the wrong direction. All that we need to do to heal any illness is to relearn how to read the body's messages and take some simple corrective actions. It is this simple. ISBN186163 1375 £11.95

FREE DETAILED CATALOGUE

Capall Bann is owned and run by people actively involved in many of the areas in which we publish. A detailed illustrated catalogue is available on request, SAE or International Postal Coupon appreciated. **Titles can be ordered direct from Capall Bann, post free in the UK** (cheque or PO with order) or from good bookshops and specialist outlets.

A Breath Behind Time, Terri Hector
Angels and Goddesses - Celtic Christianity & Paganism, M. Howard
Arthur - The Legend Unveiled, C Johnson & E Lung
Auguries and Omens - The Magical Lore of Birds, Yvonne Aburrow
Asyniur - Womens Mysteries in the Northern Tradition, S McGrath
Beginnings - Geomancy, Builder's Rites, Nigel Pennick
Between Earth and Sky, Julia Day
Book of the Veil , Peter Paddon
Caer Sidhe - Celtic Astrology and Astronomy, Michael Bayley
Call of the Horned Piper, Nigel Jackson
Cat's Company, Ann Walker
Celtic Faery Shamanism, Catrin James
Celtic Lore & Druidic Ritual, Rhiannon Ryall
Come Back To Life, Jenny Smedley
Compleat Vampyre - The Vampyre Shaman, Nigel Jackson
Creating Form From the Mist - The Wisdom of Women in Celtic Myth and
    Culture, Lynne Sinclair-Wood
Crystal Clear - A Guide to Quartz Crystal, Jennifer Dent
Crystal Doorways, Simon & Sue Lilly
Crossing the Borderlines - Guising, Masking & Ritual Animal Disguise in the
    European Tradition, Nigel Pennick
Dragons of the West, Nigel Pennick
Earth Harmony - Places of Power, Holiness & Healing, Nigel Pennick
Earth Magic, Margaret McArthur
Eildon Tree (The) Romany Language & Lore, Michael Hoadley
Enchanted Forest - The Magical Lore of Trees, Yvonne Aburrow
Eternally Yours Faithfully, Roy Radford & Evelyn Gregory
Everything You Always Wanted To Know About Your Body, But So Far
    Nobody's Been Able To Tell You, Chris Thomas & D Baker
Fairies in the Irish Tradition, Molly Gowen
Familiars - Animal Powers of Britain, Anna Franklin
Flower Wisdom, Katherine Kear
Fool's First Steps, (The) Chris Thomas

Forest Paths - Tree Divination, Brian Harrison, Ill. S. Rouse
From Past to Future Life, Dr Roger Webber
God Year, The, Nigel Pennick & Helen Field
Goddess on the Cross, Dr George Young
Goddess Year, The, Nigel Pennick & Helen Field
Goddesses, Guardians & Groves, Jack Gale
Handbook For Pagan Healers, Liz Joan
Handbook of Fairies, Ronan Coghlan
Healing Book, The, Chris Thomas and Diane Baker
Healing Homes, Jennifer Dent
Healing Journeys, Paul Williamson
Healing Stones, Sue Philips
Herb Craft - Shamanic & Ritual Use of Herbs, Lavender & Franklin
In Search of Herne the Hunter, Eric Fitch
Inner Mysteries of the Goths, Nigel Pennick
Inner Space Workbook - Develop Thru Tarot, C Summers & J Vayne
Intuitive Journey, Ann Walker Isis - African Queen, Akkadia Ford
Journey Home, The, Chris Thomas
Kecks, Keddles & Kesh - Celtic Lang & The Cog Almanac, Bayley
Legend of Robin Hood, The, Richard Rutherford-Moore
Lid Off the Cauldron, Patricia Crowther
Light From the Shadows - Modern Traditional Witchcraft, Gwyn
Lore of the Sacred Horse, Marion Davies
Magical Guardians - Exploring the Spirit and Nature of Trees, Philip Heselton
Magical History of the Horse, Janet Farrar & Virginia Russell
Magical Lore of Animals, Yvonne Aburrow
Magical Lore of Cats, Marion Davies
Magical Lore of Herbs, Marion Davies
Magick Without Peers, Ariadne Rainbird & David Rankine
Masks of Misrule - Horned God & His Cult in Europe, Nigel Jackson
Medicine For The Coming Age, Lisa Sand MD
Mind Massage - 60 Creative Visualisations, Marlene Maundrill
Mysteries of the Runes, Michael Howard
Mystic Life of Animals, Ann Walker
New Celtic Oracle The, Nigel Pennick & Nigel Jackson
Oracle of Geomancy, Nigel Pennick
Pagan Feasts - Seasonal Food for the 8 Festivals, Franklin & Phillips
Patchwork of Magic - Living in a Pagan World, Julia Day
Pathworking - A Practical Book of Guided Meditations, Pete Jennings
Personal Power, Anna Franklin
Pickingill Papers - The Origins of Gardnerian Wicca, Bill Liddell
Pillars of Tubal Cain, Nigel Jackson
Planet Earth - The Universe's Experiment, Chris Thomas
Practical Meditation, Steve Hounsome
Psychic Self Defence - Real Solutions, Jan Brodie
Real Fairies, David Tame

Reality - How It Works & Why It Mostly Doesn't, Rik Dent
Romany Tapestry, Michael Houghton
Runic Astrology, Nigel Pennick
Sacred Animals, Gordon MacLellan
Sacred Celtic Animals, Marion Davies, Ill. Simon Rouse
Sacred Dorset - On the Path of the Dragon, Peter Knight
Sacred Grove - The Mysteries of the Forest, Yvonne Aburrow
Sacred Geometry, Nigel Pennick
Sacred Ring - Pagan Origins of British Folk Festivals, M. Howard
Season of Sorcery - On Becoming a Wisewoman, Poppy Palin
Seasonal Magic - Diary of a Village Witch, Paddy Slade
Secret Places of the Goddess, Philip Heselton
Secret Signs & Sigils, Nigel Pennick
Spirits of the Earth, Jaq D Hawkins
Subterranean Kingdom, The, revised 2nd ed, Nigel Pennick
Talking to the Earth, Gordon MacLellan
Talking With Nature, Julie Hood
Taming the Wolf - Full Moon Meditations, Steve Hounsome
The Other Kingdoms Speak, Helena Hawley
Tree: Essence of Healing, Simon & Sue Lilly
Understanding Chaos Magic, Jaq D Hawkins
Water Witches, Tony Steele
Way of the Magus, Michael Howard
Weaving a Web of Magic, Rhiannon Ryall
West Country Wicca, Rhiannon Ryall
Wheel of the Year, Teresa Moorey & Jane Brideson
Wildwitch - The Craft of the Natural Psychic, Poppy Palin
Wildwood King , Philip Kane
Wondrous Land - The Faery Faith of Ireland by Dr Kay Mullin
Working With the Merlin, Geoff Hughes
Understanding Past Lives, Dilys Gater
Understanding Second Sight, Dilys Gater
Understanding Spirit Guides, Dilys Gater
Understanding Star Children, Dilys Gater
The Urban Shaman, Dilys Gater
Your Talking Pet, Ann Walker